The Contradictions *of* "Real Socialism"

The Conductor and the Conducted

by MICHAEL A. LEBOWITZ

MR

MONTHLY REVIEW PRESS

New York

Library of Congress Cataloging-in-Publication Data
Lebowitz, Michael A.
  The contradictions of real socialism : the conductor and the conducted /
by Michael A. Lebowitz.
      p. cm.
  Includes bibliographical references and index.
  ISBN 978-1-58367-256-3 (pbk. : alk. paper) — ISBN 978-1-58367-257-0
(cloth : alk. paper) 1. Communism. 2. Socialism. I. Title.
  HX73.L4163 2012
  335—dc23

                        2012019992

Monthly Review Press
146 West 29th Street, Suite 6W
New York, New York 10001

www.monthlyreview.org

5 4 3 2 1

Praise for *The Contradictions of 'Real Socialism'*

"The owl of Minerva only flies at dusk"—it was Hegel's old maxim that seemed confirmed when in 1991 the *Socialist Register* published Michael Lebowitz's article on the nature of "real socialism" amid its very demise. This new book takes off from there, but its wings are buoyed by Lebowitz's work since then, from *Beyond Capital* to *The Socialist Alternative*. The profound understanding in this new book of why twentieth-century attempts at constructing socialism failed must be an essential element in the socialist renewal emerging amid the first great capitalist crisis of the twenty-first century. It thus appears that the old wise owl also flies at dawn.

—LEO PANITCH, editor, *Socialist Register*

If we want socialism for the twenty-first century, we need to understand why the "real" socialisms of the last century so often ended in capitalism. In this book, Lebowitz shows, theoretically and historically, that the socialism practiced in the Soviet Union and Central Europe was doomed because vanguard relations of production weakened the working class, ensuring that it would have no primary role in the battle ultimately won by the logic of capital (represented by managers) over the logic of the vanguard (represented by the party). We must, he concludes, reject vanguard Marxism and embrace a Marxist vision of socialism in which, from the beginning, the full development of human capacities is actively promoted. There is a lot to learn here.

—MARTIN HART-LANDSBERG, professor of economics,
Lewis and Clark College

One doesn't have to agree with all the theses presented in Michael Lebowitz's latest book in order to acknowledge that this is a major contribution to the international debate on socialism of the twenty-first century. Drawing lessons from the dramatic failure of so-called "real socialism," he argues, with powerful and persuasive logic, that a new society, based on values of solidarity and community, cannot be created by a state standing over and above civil society: only through autonomous organizations—at the neighborhood, community, and national levels—can people transform both circumstances and themselves.

—MICHAEL LÖWY, co-author, *Che Guevara: His Revolutionary Legacy*
(with Olivier Besancenot)

What would Marx have thought had he lived to see the Soviet Union? Nobody has interpreted Marx to greater advantage to answer this question than renowned Marxist scholar Michael Lebowitz, who explains in *The Contradictions of 'Real Socialism'* why Marx would not have been pleased!

—ROBIN HAHNEL, professor of economics, Portland State University

We need this well-written book to understand that socialism did not die with the fall of the Berlin Wall.

—FRANÇOIS HOUTART, Executive Secretary of
the World Forum for Alternatives

Where fresh insights are rare, indeed, Michael Lebowitz provides a bundle of them. Although no one will (or perhaps should) agree with everything here, the book provides rich material for badly-needed discussion.

—PAUL BUHLE, author, *Marxism in the United States*

A riveting exploration of what can be learned from the first attempts to create socialist systems, specifically the period from 1950 through the 1980s. Lebowitz convincingly demonstrates that the distortions of the model developed in the Soviet Union and copied in eastern European countries ("real socialism") were caused by setting in motion two contradictory forces—ending up with the worst aspects of both capital and leadership and control by a "vanguard." He examines the development of "real socialism" as a complex system, with the various parts explained and scrutinized in their interactions and interrelations as part of the system. Required reading for those interested in avoiding diversions and pitfalls in a post capitalist alternative—on the path to creating a system under social, instead of private, control in which the goal is meeting everyone's basic needs and encouraging and allowing the full human development of all.

—FRED MAGDOFF, professor emeritus of plant and soil science,
University of Vermont

Contents

For friends in Cuba, Venezuela,

and everywhere people are struggling to build a new world.

Hasta la victoria siempre!

Preface

This is not a book for those who already know everything important there is to know about "Real Socialism." For those fortunate souls who have inherited or adopted the eternal verities of particular political sects on the left, empirical footnotes that strengthen their claim to leadership are the principal tasks of scholarship. As a result, the central question about this book for them is likely to be, "Is he with us or against us?" In short, is this book good for the chosen?

I presume, however, readers who begin with questions rather than answers. What was this phenomenon known as "Real Socialism," or "Actually Existing Socialism," a concept created in the twentieth century by the leaders of countries in order to distinguish their real experience from merely theoretical socialist ideas? What were its characteristics? How was this system reproduced? And why did it ultimately yield to capitalism without resistance from the working classes who were presumably its beneficiaries?

I didn't plan to write this book. My original idea was to include a few chapters on "Real Socialism" in my book *The Socialist Alternative: Real Human Development*, published by Monthly Review Press in 2010. The point I wanted to make is that the socialist alternative is an alternative not only to capitalism but also to "Real Socialism." However, after drafting a few chapters based in particular on the experience of the Soviet Union and Eastern Europe, I realized that this section of the book was "taking over" and demanded a book of its own. So, as I indicated in the Preface to *The Socialist Alternative,* I decided to shift this material plus a discussion of the Yugoslav experience with market self-management to a separate project, which I called "studies in the development of socialism."

In my attempt to apply Marx's methodology to the study of Real Socialism (hereafter noted without quotation marks), however, I found myself constantly surprised because the subject under investigation continually revealed new sides that had to be explored, sides that I hadn't considered in my years of teaching the subject. As a result, the book grew in size and took much longer to complete than anticipated. And, its scope was reduced. First to go was the discussion of the Yugoslav experience, now put off to a future project. But in addition, the discussion of Real Socialism as such was itself truncated.

Originally, my plan was to analyze Real Socialism as a system that consolidated in the period after 1950 and then to follow that with a section on its historical development. My model in this respect was Marx's treatment of capitalism in *Capital,* which revealed the nature of capitalism as a going system (its "being") and then used that analysis as a guideline for examining the original emergence of the system (its "becoming"). So, Part I would explore the nature of a system dominated by what I have called "vanguard relations of production," whereas Part II would consider the original emergence (or original accumulation) of those relations.

Accordingly, the chapters drafted for Part II took up topics like the emergence of the vanguard party in the USSR, NEP (the New Economic Policy), social relations within the countryside, and the theory of "primitive socialist accumulation." Only the discussion of the 1930s remained to be done. But these questions, too, have been set aside for another work, for now.

This is not at all a book without premises. As the Introduction reveals, I start from an understanding that at the core of socialism is a focus upon human development, upon, indeed, the development of human capacities, a process inseparable from human activity. But that specter is not the subject matter of this book. We understand Real Socialism best, I suggest, not by proceeding from theory and the simple application of concepts from the study of capitalism but by beginning, as Marx did, from the real, concrete phenomena of these societies and by trying to grasp the underlying structure that generates them.

Our examination of Real Socialism begins by investigating an omnipresent characteristic in the system—shortages. To understand the factors underlying the "shortage economy," we consider first the concept of a particular social contract that offered some definite benefits for the working class, and then we explore the character of vanguard relations of production. But there was more to Real Socialism than one set of relations. We see an inherent struggle between the logic of the vanguard and the logic of capital; in addition, we see a particular set of beliefs on the part of the working class (the moral economy of the working class in Real Socialism), which provides glimpses of an alternative logic, the logic of the working class. Can the latter be built upon in Real Socialism? That is the question for which we provide some suggestions but no definitive answer.

Although the focus is to move from concrete phenomena to an understanding of those phenomena, we begin the book with two abstract sections. Firstly, the Introduction presents my premises about capitalism and the concept of socialism for the twenty-first century. In this respect, it provides a bridge between the discussion in *The Socialist Alternative* and this book. Secondly, "The Overture" introduces the question of the conductor and the conducted (the subtitle of this book). It specifically poses a question about the need for a "directing authority" and the issue of power. Indeed, the Overture introduces the leitmotif of the book: the possibility of socialism in a society divided into conductor and conducted.

Once again, I need to point out that this book owes much to the encouragement, commitment, and comradeship of my partner Marta Harnecker (whose work ethic makes my reputed workaholism appear like the behavior of a sloth). I have benefited much, too, from David Mandel, who has read several parts of this book and has offered useful critical comments. Finally, especially encouraging (and daunting) have been messages from a number of people who have told me how much they are looking forward to this book. I hope that I have raised the right questions for them.

—Michael A. Lebowitz, March 25, 2012

Bishop, I can fly,
The tailor said to the Bishop.
Just watch how it works.
And he climbed with things
That looked like wings
To the broad, broad roof of the church.
The Bishop passed by.
It's all a lie,
Man is no bird,
No one will ever fly,
The Bishop said of the tailor.

The tailor is done for,
The people said to the Bishop.
It was the talk of the fair.
His wings were smashed
And he was dashed
On the hard, hard stones of the square.
Toll the bells in the steeple,
It was all a lie,
Man is no bird,
No one will ever fly,
The Bishop said to the people.

—BERTOLT BRECHT [1]

New Wings for Socialism

In 1990, I began an essay (bearing the subtitle "A Cautionary Tale") with Brecht's poem about the tailor who put on "things that looked like wings," climbed to the roof of a church, tried to fly, and crashed.[2] In 1990, what many called the socialist world crashed.[3] And, everywhere there were experts who saw this as proof: socialism had failed. *No one will ever fly.*

What I attempted to do in that essay was to challenge the theoretical arguments against socialism, theoretical arguments in particular against the Marxist case for socialism. And I proposed that there had been a distortion of Marxism both in theory and in practice—a distortion that forgot about human beings, a determinist message focusing upon productive forces that was silent about "the nature of human beings produced within an economic system." The determinist argument that stresses the primacy of productive forces, I argued, could never understand why Marx sacrificed his "health, happiness and family" to write *Capital*. Nor could it make sense of why Marx never stopped stressing that workers can make themselves fit to create a new society only through the process of struggle.

What was my essential point? It was to emphasize the importance of developing a new common sense—one that sees the logic of producing together to satisfy human needs. The failure to do this and to stress instead the development of productive forces, I proposed, leads inevitably to a dead end—the dead end that we could see in front of us. The point was simple: as Che Guevara stressed, to build socialism it is essential, along with building new material foundations, to build new human beings.

But how? I focused upon a number of elements. Self-management in the process of production, I argued, was an essential element: "Insofar as people produce themselves in the course of all their activities, the very process of engaging in democratic forms of production is an essential part of producing people for whom the need for cooperation is second nature." But self-management in particular productive units is not sufficient. You need, I argued, to replace a focus on selfishness and self-orientation with a focus on community and solidarity, a conscious emphasis upon human needs; that is, the necessity to engage in collective solutions to satisfy human needs must be "recognised as a responsibility of all individuals." And, producing people with these characteristics could never be achieved by a state standing over and above civil society. "Rather, only through their own activities through autonomous organisations—at the neighbourhood, community and national levels—can people transform both circumstances and themselves." What, in short, was necessary was "the conscious development of a socialist civil society."

Thus I stressed the centrality of human beings and the development of the institutions that permit them to transform themselves. This had not occurred in the Soviet model. "With its lack of democratic and cooperative production, its absence of a socialist civil society and its actually existing bureaucratic rule," Real Socialism had not produced the new human beings who could build a better world. And that, I proposed, was the lesson we had to learn from this experience. Rather than concluding from the crash that socialism had failed and that no one would ever fly, the lesson for socialists was different. My concluding line was: "No one should ever again try to fly with those things that only *look* like wings."

In the Absence of an Alternative

A lot has occurred since 1990 when that essay was written. However, one thing that has not changed is that, now as then, the absence of a vision of a socialist alternative ensures that there is no alternative to capitalism. If you don't know where you want to go, no road will take you there. The result is that you end up going nowhere—or, more precisely, your struggles are either defeated or absorbed within capitalism.

For many critics of capitalism, though, the system is on the verge of collapse. It is fragile—requiring for some only a cacophony of loud "*No*'s or a resounding chorus of "silent farts" for it to crumble.[4] For others, since capitalism is about to enter its final economic crisis (or, indeed, has been in it for decades), it is time to document the dying days of this doomed system.[5] But for Marx, it was *not* so simple—capitalism was not fragile. Despite his hatred of a system that exploited and destroyed both human beings and nature, he understood that capitalism is strong and that it tends to create the conditions for its reproduction as a system.

Capitalism is a system centered upon a relationship between capitalists, owners of the means of production who are driven by the desire for profits (surplus value), and workers who are separated from means of production and who have no alternative to maintain themselves but to sell their capacity to perform labor (labor-power). But how, Marx asked, does such a system reproduce itself? How are its premises produced and reproduced?

From the side of capital, this is easy to understand. Through its purchase of labor-power, capital obtains both the right to direct workers in the labor process as well as property rights to what the worker produces. It uses these rights to exploit workers (that is, to compel the performance of surplus labor) and thus to produce commodities that contain surplus value. What capital wants, though, is not those impregnated commodities but to make real that surplus value in the form of money by selling those commodities.

With the successful sale of those commodities (and, thus, the realization of the surplus value), capital is able to renew the means of production consumed in the process of production, hire wage-laborers again, maintain its own desired consumption and accumulate capital for the purpose of expansion. However, capital's ability to continue to operate as capital requires the reproduction of workers as wage-laborers (that is, as workers who reappear in the labor market to sell their labor-power in order to survive). But what ensures this? While capital constantly tries to drive wages down, workers push in the opposite direction. So what ensures that workers will not gain sufficient wages to extract themselves from the need to sell their ability to work in order to survive?[6]

One way capital keeps wages down is by dividing and separating workers so they compete against each other rather than combine against capital. Not only can capital do this by using workers against each other (as Marx described the way capital took advantage of the hostility between English and Irish workers) but also it constantly reproduces a reserve army of the unemployed by substituting machinery for workers. The competition among workers and the division into employed and unemployed both tend to keep wages down. "The great beauty of capitalist production," Marx commented, is that by producing "a relative surplus population of wage-labourers," wages are "confined within limits satisfactory to capitalist exploitation, and lastly, the social dependence of the worker on the capitalist, which is indispensable, is secured."[7]

Yet Marx offered an additional reason for the reproduction of wage-labor (and thus the reproduction of capitalist relations of production). Workers are not only exploited within capitalist relations—they are also *deformed*. If we forget this second side of capitalist oppression, we can never understand why workers fail to rise up when capital enters into one of its many crises. We need, in short, to understand the nature of the workers produced within capitalism.

While capital develops productive forces to achieve its preconceived goal (the growth of profits and capital), Marx pointed out that "all means for the development of production" under capitalism "distort the worker into a fragment of a man," degrade him and "alienate him from the intellectual potentialities of the labour process."[8] *Capital* explains the mutilation, the impoverishment, the "crippling of body and mind" of the worker "bound hand and foot for life to a single specialized operation" that occurs in the division of labor characteristic of the capitalist process of manufacturing. But did the development of machinery permit workers to develop their capabilities? The possibility was present but in capitalism this *completed* the "separation of the intellectual faculties of the production process from manual labour."[9] In short, thinking and doing become separate and hostile, and "every atom of freedom, both in bodily and in intellectual activity" is lost.

A particular type of person is produced within capitalism. Producing within capitalist relations is a process of a "complete emptying-out," "total alienation," the "sacrifice of the human end-in-itself to an entirely external end."[10] How else but with money, the true need that capitalism creates, can we fill the vacuum? We fill the vacuum of our lives with *things*—we are driven to consume. In addition to producing commodities and capital itself, capitalism produces a fragmented, crippled human being, whose enjoyment consists in possessing and consuming things. More and more things. Capital constantly generates new needs for workers and it is upon this that "the contemporary power of capital rests"; every new need for capitalist commodities is a new link in the golden chain that links workers to capital.[11]

Is it likely, then, that people produced within capitalism can spontaneously grasp the nature of this destructive system? On the contrary, the inherent tendency of capital is to produce people who think that there is no alternative. Marx was clear that capital tends to produce the working class it *needs*, workers who treat capitalism as common sense:

> The advance of capitalist production develops a working class which by education, tradition and habit looks upon the requirement of that mode of production as self-evident natural laws. The organization of the capitalist process of production, once it is fully developed, breaks down all resistance.[12]

Breaks down all resistance! And Marx proceeded to add that capital's generation of a reserve army of the unemployed "puts the seal on the domination of the capitalist over the worker" and that the capitalist can rely upon the worker's "dependence on capital, which springs from the conditions of production themselves, and is guaranteed in perpetuity by them."[13] Obviously, for Marx, capital's walls will never crumble with a loud scream.

Of course, workers *do* struggle against capital for specific goals—they struggle for better wages, workdays of lower length and intensity and for benefits that will allow them to satisfy more of their needs within this wage-labor relation. However, no matter how much they may struggle on particular questions such as questions of "fairness" (for example, "fair" wages, "fair" day's work), as long as workers look upon the requirements of capitalism "as self-evident natural laws," those struggles occur within the bounds of the capitalist relation. In the end, their subordination to the logic of capital means that faced with capitalism's crises, they sooner or later act to ensure the conditions for the reproduction of capital.

And *that* is why Marx wrote *Capital.* Precisely because of capital's inherent tendency to develop a working class that looks upon capital's requirements as common sense, Marx's purpose was to explain the nature of capital to workers and to help them to understand the necessity to go beyond capitalism.[14] Understanding that capitalism is a perverse society that deforms people and that capital itself is the result of exploitation, however, is *not* enough. If people think there is no alternative, then they will struggle to do their best within capitalism but will not waste their time and energy trying to achieve the impossible.

Here is why the story of the fall of Real Socialism is so important. It serves as a "cautionary tale"—socialism, we are told, cannot succeed. It was all a lie. No one will ever fly. There is no alternative. For so many, the story of Real Socialism killed the idea of a socialist alternative.

As Marx understood, ideas become a material force when they grasp the minds of masses. For many years, as the result of characteristics of Real Socialism (as well as its ultimate fall), people unhappy with capitalism have been convinced there is no alternative, that the logic of capital is common sense and that, accordingly, the best hope is capitalism with a human face. The result has been to strengthen capitalism.

For this reason, to understand Real Socialism and why it crashed is not an exercise in the study of history (like the study of feudalism). Rather, we know now—more clearly than in 1990—that there *must* be an alternative. There must be an alternative to a system that by its very nature involves a spiral of growing alienated production, growing needs and growing consumption—a pattern the earth cannot sustain. The specter we face is that of barbarism—not only because of the limits of the earth (reflected in the evidence of global warming and the growing shortages that reflect rising demands for the earth's resources) but also because of the growing competition for those resources—a competition not likely to be left to the market.

A New Vision:
Socialism for the Twenty-first Century

There is, though, a new vision of socialism that has emerged in the twenty-first century as an alternative to barbarism. At its core is the alternative that Marx evoked in *Capital*: in contrast to a society in which the worker exists to satisfy the need of capital for its growth, Marx pointed to "the inverse situation, in which objective wealth is there to satisfy the worker's own need for development." Human development, in short, is at the center of this vision of the alternative to capitalism.[15]

From his early discussion of a "rich human being" to his later comments about the "development of the rich individuality which is as all-sided in its production as in its consumption," the "development of all human powers as such the end in itself" and "the all-around development of the individual," Marx focused upon our need for the full development of our capacities; this is the essence of his conception of socialism—a society that removes all obstacles to the full development of human beings.[16]

But Marx always understood that human development requires practice. It does not come as a gift from above. His concept of "revolutionary practice," that concept of "the coincidence of the changing of circumstances and of human activity or self-change," is the red thread that runs throughout his work.[17] In every process of human activity, there is more than one product of labor. Starting from his articulation of the concept of "revolutionary practice," Marx consistently stressed that, through their activity, people simultaneously change as they change circumstances.

We develop ourselves, in short, through our own practice and are the products of all our activities—the products of our struggles (or the lack of same), the products of all the relations in which we produce and interact. In every human activity, in short, there is a *joint product*—both the change in the object of labor and the change in the laborer herself.[18]

Marx's unity of human development and practice constitutes the *key link* we need to grasp if we are to talk about socialism. What kind of productive relations can provide the conditions for the full development of human capacities? Only those in which there is conscious cooperation among associated producers; only those in which the goal of production is that of the workers themselves. Worker management that ends the division between thinking and doing is essential—but clearly this requires more than worker management in individual workplaces. They must be the goals of workers in society, too—workers in their communities.

Implicit in the emphasis upon this key link of human development and practice, accordingly, is our need to be able to develop through democratic, participatory and protagonistic activity in every aspect of our lives. Through revolutionary practice in our communities, our workplaces, and in all our social institutions, we produce ourselves as "rich human beings"—rich in capacities and needs—in contrast to the impoverished and crippled human beings that capitalism produces. This concept is one of democracy *in* practice, democracy *as* practice, *democracy as protagonism*. Democracy in this sense—protagonistic democracy in the workplace, protagonistic democracy in neighborhoods, communities, communes—is the democracy of people who are transforming themselves into revolutionary subjects.

We are describing here one element in the concept of socialism for the twenty-first century—a concept of socialism as a particular organic system of production, distribution and consumption. *Social production organized by workers* is essential for developing the capacities of producers and building new relations—relations of cooperation and solidarity. And if workers do not make decisions in their workplaces and communities and develop their capacities, we can be certain that *someone else will*. In short, protagonistic democracy in all our workplaces is an essential condition for the full development of the producers.

But there are other elements in this socialist combination. The society we want to build is one that recognizes that "the free development of each is the condition for the free development of all." How can we ensure, though, that our communal, social productivity is directed to the free development of *all* rather than used to satisfy the private goals of capitalists, groups of individuals, or state bureaucrats? A second side of what President Chavez of Venezuela called on his *Alo Presidente* program in January 2007 the "elementary triangle of socialism" concerns the distribution of the means of production.[19] *Social ownership of the means of production* is that second side. Of course, it is essential to understand that social ownership is not the same as state ownership. Social ownership implies a profound democracy—one in which people function as subjects, both as producers and as members of society, in determining the use of the results of our social labor.

Are common ownership of the means of production and cooperation in the process of production, however, sufficient for "ensuring overall human development"? What kind of people are produced when we relate to others through an exchange relation and try to get the best deal possible for ourselves? This brings us to the third side of the triangle: *satisfaction of communal needs and communal purposes.* Here, the focus is upon the importance of basing our productive activity upon the recognition of our common humanity and our needs as members of the human family. In short, the premise is the development of a solidarian society— one in which we go beyond self-interest and where, through our activity, we both build solidarity among people and at the same time produce ourselves differently.

These three sides of the "socialist triangle" form members of a whole. They are parts of a "structure in which all the elements coexist simultaneously and support one another"—an organic system of production, distribution, and consumption. Associated producers working with socially owned products of past labor to produce for social needs reproduce their conditions of existence through their activity.[20] "In the completed bourgeois system," Marx commented about capitalism, "every economic relation presupposes every other in its bourgeois economic form, and everything posited is thus also a presupposition; this is the case with every organic system."[21] It is also true of socialism as an organic system: every economic relation presupposes every other in its socialist economic form in the completed socialist system.

THINGS THAT ONLY LOOK LIKE WINGS

This book, however, is not about the theory of socialism as an organic system. Rather, it is about that attempt in the twentieth century to build an alternative to capitalism, an alternative that relied upon things that looked like wings and which crashed.

But, what were those things that looked like wings? For some people, the cautionary tale is all about state ownership of means of production. Accordingly, to escape the fate of Real Socialism, they argue that we must accept that private ownership of means of production is essential. For others, the tale revolves around the reliance in Real Socialism upon central planning. So, their answer is that markets are not specific to capitalism and that a viable alternative to capitalism must embrace the market.

If we are skeptical about such conclusions, though, what is our alternative explanation for the fate of Real Socialism? To select and blame a *different* element from the combination that made up Real Socialism—for example, underdeveloped capitalism, the lack of world revolution, short men with moustaches? That can be an entertaining parlor game but in the absence of a careful consideration of precisely how various elements within Real Socialism were interconnected and interacted to make up that whole, can we really understand its fate? Which were inherent, indeed necessary, aspects and which were contingent, merely historical elements?

To understand the significance of individual elements, we need to try to understand Real Socialism as a system. Even elements that correspond to what may be found in capitalism or to the concept of socialism for the twenty-first century by themselves are not sufficient to identify the nature of the system. Parts, after all, gain their significance from the particular combinations in which they exist—that is, the whole of which they are part. Even *real* wings are only parts.

The Conductor and the Conducted

Do we need leaders? Certainly, when we work together on a common project, we are more productive than when we are separate and isolated. The whole is greater than the sum of the parts taken individually. But do we need a director in order to work together on a common project?

A Directing Authority

Within capitalist relations of production, a capitalist hires "individual, isolated" owners of labor-power, directs their cooperation and owns the products of their collective labor. As the owner of the result of their activity, he is the beneficiary of "the social productive power which arises from cooperation"; it is "a *free gift*" to that capitalist.[1] According to Marx, though, direction in the process of cooperation is not unique to capitalism: "All directly social or communal labour on a large-scale requires, to a greater or lesser degree, a directing authority." He offered two reasons: (a) "in order to secure a harmonious cooperation of the activities of individuals" and (b) "to perform the general functions that have their origin in the motion of the total productive organism, as distinguished from the motion of its separate organs."[2]

According to Marx, in short, there is a *general* necessity for the "function of direction which arises out of the nature of the communal labour process." That general requirement, though, must not be confused with the particular content and form that it takes on within capitalism. After all, the essence of capitalist direction embodies capital's drive to expand surplus value (thus the greatest possible exploitation of workers), the need to overcome the resistance of workers and the need to protect investments in the means of production. Accordingly, capitalist direction is inherently an *antagonistic* process, and it takes on "despotic" forms—a hierarchy of supervisors whose function is to police workers and command in the name of capital.[3]

But a despotic character of direction is not unique to capitalism. "In all modes of production that are based on opposition of the worker as direct producer and the proprietor of the means of production," supervision and control of the producers is essential. Marx pointed to, for example, the supervision of slaves in the Roman Empire and also to "despotic states," where "supervision and all-round intervention of the government" involves "the specific functions that arise from the opposition between the government and the mass of the people."[4] In all such cases, direction is "twofold in content"—it is general and specific, both that aspect related to every socially combined labor process and also that specific aspect related to maintenance of the particular character of exploitation.[5]

Let us try, though, to separate these two aspects logically and to consider in itself the *general* side—that "work of supervision and management [that] necessarily arises where the direct production process takes the form of a socially combined process, and does not appear simply as the isolated labour of separate producers." According to Marx, this combined labor in itself is enough to require a "directing authority": "where many individuals cooperate," he noted, "the interconnection and unity of the process is necessarily represented in a governing will, and in functions that concern not the detailed work but rather the workplace and its activity as the whole, as with the conductor of an orchestra."[6] In a process of cooperation, someone must have responsibility for the whole, for "the total productive organism."

For Marx, the orchestra conductor was a symbol of directing authority that is not based upon the division between producers and the owners of the means of production. The conductor does not lead the orchestra because he owns the means of production: "A musical conductor," Marx writes, "need in no way be the owner of the instruments in his orchestra"; rather, his role as leader is the result of "the productive functions that all combined social labour assigns to particular individuals as their special work."[7] In short, the orchestra conductor is *necessary*. "A single violin player is his own conductor; an orchestra requires a separate one."[8]

The "special work" assigned to the orchestra conductor is to see the members of this orchestra as a whole rather than as a collection of separate players and to ensure that they function harmoniously and successfully as a unit in performing the predetermined score. Thus the conductor articulates the separate powers of the individual musicians into a collective power, where the whole is greater than the sum of its individual parts. But to secure that "harmonious cooperation" and to function as the agent of the whole, the conductor must be able to exercise authority over the individual members.

Does the conductor, then, have power over the members of the orchestra? For Elias Canetti, the conductor is the *embodiment* of power:

> His eyes hold the whole orchestra. Every player feels that the conductor sees him personally, and still more, hears him. The voices of the instruments are opinions and convictions on which he keeps a close watch. He is omniscient, for, while the players have only their own parts in front of them, he has the whole score in his head, or on his desk. At any given moment he knows precisely what each player should be doing. His attention is everywhere at once, and it is to this that he owes a large part of his authority. He is inside the mind of every player. He knows not only what each *should* be doing, but also what he *is* doing. He is the living embodiment of law, both positive and negative. His hands decree and prohibit. His ears search out profanation.[9]

Truly, this is power: "Quite small movements are all he needs to wake this or that instrument to life or to silence it at will. He has the power of life and death over the voices of the instruments; one long silent will speak again at his command." To be able to exercise that power, on the other hand, requires that the players accept those commands: "The willingness of its members to obey him makes it possible for the conductor to transform them into a unit, which he then embodies."[10]

In this description of the orchestra, there is no room for spontaneity or improvisation. Rather, the predetermined score must be followed. In this division of labor, each player has a precise assignment. By performing their assigned tasks with the regularity of a machine and by following the directives of the conductor, the orchestra as a whole achieves the result that exists ideally in the mind (or on the desk) of the conductor.

THE "KEY LINK":
HUMAN DEVELOPMENT AND PRACTICE

But, as we noted earlier, there is always more than one product of human activity. When we grasp the "key link" of human development and practice, we understand that every labor process inside and outside the formal process of production has as its result a *joint product*—both the change in the object of labor and the change in the laborer herself.

If this is the case, then, we always need to ask not only about the success of a labor process in achieving a particular predetermined goal but also about the nature of the human beings and capacities produced within the process. When the capacities of workers grow through their activity, this is an essential investment in human beings. Accordingly, in my book *The Socialist Alternative* I argue that "socialist accountancy" and a concept of "socialist efficiency" must incorporate explicitly the effects upon human capacities of all activities.[11]

Marx explored this question at length in *Capital*—by demonstrating the *negative* effect upon the capacities of workers of production under capitalist relations. He pointed out that under the direction of capital, the producers are subordinated to a plan drawn up by the capitalist, and their activity is subjected to his authority and purpose; the joint product that emerges from this particular social labor process separates thinking and doing, and its results must be entered as negative in any accounting system that values human development.[12]

This is what we need to keep clearly in mind when we think about socialism. Social production organized by workers is a necessary condition for the full development of the producers; it is not something to be put off to some future society. "As long as workers are prevented from developing their capacities by combining thinking and doing in the workplace, they remain alienated and fragmented human beings whose enjoyment consists in possessing and consuming things."[13] Once we grasp Marx's insight into revolutionary practice, the importance of that key link of human development and practice, we recognize that the process of building socialism must be one of simultaneously producing new socialist human beings—that is, *two* products rather than one.

Return, though, to Marx's metaphor for the general necessity for a directing authority where many individuals cooperate—the orchestra conductor. Think about how that particular conductor enforces the division of labor of the players (including the separation of thinking and doing) in order for them to perform the predetermined score as a harmonious unit; and think about what he *rejects*—spontaneous creation, collective interaction among the players, jazz.

The orchestra performs the music. But what is the joint product in this process? What development of human capacities occurs in this social labor process under the direction of the orchestra conductor as described above? Certainly, this process is far more rewarding than isolated, individual activity: "When the worker co-operates in a planned way with others, he strips off the fetters of his individuality, and develops the capabilities of his species."[14] Certainly, too, the members of the orchestra can take pride in their collective accomplishment.

But when they are working in accordance with the plan of another who stands over and above them and are subjected to a strict division of labor, what the collective worker achieves occurs at the expense of the individual member. As in the case of the division of labor that developed in manufacture, "the knowledge, judgement and will" otherwise exercised by an individual musician is now concentrated in this relation in the representative of the whole.[15] What individuals lose in this process is the opportunity to develop their own capacities by exercising their knowledge, judgment and will collectively.

Compare this to a process in which the musicians listen to each other, engage in conversation and build upon the contributions of each other. That is a process in which the whole exceeds the sum of the parts taken individually and where the capacities of the producers expand through their practice. Leadership in such cases, to a greater or lesser extent, involves general guidance and the space for initiative from below; its joint product is demonstrated by the emergence of *new* leaders.

SERVE THE MUSIC

Do we need leaders? There is a great difference between the recognition of the importance of coordination, on the one hand, and the conclusion that leadership is "the special work" assigned to particular individuals on the other. The first flows from understanding the benefits of social cooperation and is not specific to any form of coordination. The second involves a particular division of labor—*a social relation in which the roles of conductor and conducted are fixed, and commands flow one way.*

A general process of direction of combined labor is an abstraction. Coordination always occurs "within and through a specific form of society," and the example of the orchestra conductor identified by Marx is one form (but *only* one form) of non-capitalist direction.[16] To demystify the nature of capital, it was sufficient for Marx to point to the orchestra conductor to demonstrate that capitalists as such are not necessary as functionaries of production. That, however, does not mean that the relation of conductor and conducted is the appropriate form of cooperation in the society of associated producers.[17]

There are different forms of leadership and different goals. If people are produced through their activity within particular relations, the human products of a society divided into conductors and the conducted will be specific to that society. And how is such a society reproduced? Will those who receive commands from the conductor *always* need particular individuals who have the power to direct as their "special work"? And how are those who exercise power chosen and produced?

Consider the conductor. If we are to believe Canetti, the conductor does not seek power for personal gain or for the exercise of power itself. Rather, the music is "the only thing that counts ... and no one is more convinced of this than the conductor himself." To transform an assemblage of different people into a unit, to monitor all closely, to ensure that they all play their parts properly, to silence those who deviate from the plan—no one is more convinced than the conductor "that his business is to serve music and to interpret it faithfully."[18] I am essential, he thinks—without me, there would be chaos.

Metaphors can be dangerous—they can illuminate for a moment but can never substitute for analysis.[19] To understand "real socialism," we need to go beyond metaphor.

1—The Shortage Economy

Let us begin by identifying the object of study. Real Socialism as a concept emerged in the 1970s in the Soviet Union and Eastern Europe for the principal purpose of distinguishing the existing system there from theoretical or abstract concepts of socialism. Critiques of capitalism, it was argued, could no longer be "confined to the purely conceptual realm. They are impelled by the rich experience of countries that have successfully built (or are building) socialism." In short, there was a developed socialism, "a really existing socialist society," a new society that had been built as the result of real practice.[1]

The development of this concept of Real Socialism played several roles. Firstly, it served as a means to defend against criticism of the Soviet model by those who harkened back to Marx and Engels, those who argued the need for reforms (for example, those who looked for "socialism with a human face") as well as those who thought they could build socialism by a different way (as in China at the time).[2] There was another function as well: this concept of Real Socialism allowed the Brezhnev leadership to distinguish their focus from the stress in the preceding Khrushchev period upon building communism. Real Socialism was still to be understood as a stage of history preceding communism; however, it needed to be understood as a consolidated, stable system and celebrated as such.

For our purpose, then, Real Socialism refers to the nature of the system in the Soviet Union and in the countries in Eastern and Central Europe that adopted the Soviet model in the period roughly from the 1950s through the 1980s. Thus our principal focus is upon the system which was more or less consolidated and stable rather than the original emergence of that system.[3]

THE SYSTEM PARADIGM

To consider Real Socialism as a system, the appropriate starting point is with Marx—"the pioneer of the system paradigm" according to Janos Kornai, the Hungarian analyst of Real Socialism. "Researchers who think in terms of the system paradigm," Kornai proposes, "are concerned with the system as a whole, and with the relations between the whole and its parts."[4] That certainly was what Marx did. Considering the concept of an organic system, a "structure of society, in which all relations coexist simultaneously and support one another," Marx stressed that its elements could not be treated as "independent, autonomous neighbours" extrinsically or accidentally related; rather, they "all form the members of a totality, distinctions within a unity."[5]

This focus upon the whole constitutes a methodological revolution.[6] It breaks with the "Cartesian" heritage that views the parts as "ontologically prior to the whole; that is, the parts exist in isolation and come together to make wholes." In that Cartesian paradigm, described brilliantly by Levins and Lewontin, "the parts have intrinsic properties, which they possess in isolation and which they lend to the whole." In Marx's dialectical perspective, by contrast, the parts have *no* prior independent existence as parts. They "acquire properties by virtue of being parts of a particular whole, properties they do not have in isolation or as parts of another whole."[7]

In addition to situating parts within particular wholes, the system paradigm leads us to think about how systems change. "What distinguishes the thinking of those working within the system paradigm from that of their colleagues outside it," Kornai argues, "is that they are interested in the *big* changes, in the big transformations. For instance, they enquire into what processes of decay are going on within a system, so that it will come to an end and give way to another system. They ask how there occurs a transition from one system to another system, or from one typical version of a great system to another."[8]

But we also must ask, why do systems *not* change? Why did slavery last for centuries? Why did feudalism? And what keeps capitalism going? How is it that tomorrow there are capitalists and wage laborers? What makes these relations stable? In short, when you focus upon systems, you ask both what permits the reproduction of a system and also what leads to its non-reproduction.

The Reproduction of Economic Systems

"Whatever the social form of production process," Marx declared at the opening of chapter 23 of volume 1 of *Capital*, "it has to be continuous; it must periodically repeat the same phases. A society can no more cease to produce than it can cease to consume. When viewed, therefore, as a connected whole, and in the constant flux of its incessant renewal, every social process of production is at the same time a process of reproduction."[9]

Following that opening general statement, Marx demonstrated that his specific discussion in *Capital* had provided the basis for viewing capitalism as a system of reproduction. He underlined this point by concluding the chapter as follows:

> The capitalist process of production, therefore, seen as a total, connected process, i.e. a process of reproduction, produces not only commodities, not only surplus value, but also produces and reproduces the capital-relation itself; on one hand the capitalist, on the other the wage-labourer.[10]

The subject, thus, was a "connected whole" constantly in the process of renewal—one that produces and reproduces material products and social relations—which are themselves presuppositions and premises of production. "Those conditions, like these relations, are on the one hand the presuppositions of the capitalist production process, on the other its results and creations; they are both produced and reproduced by it."[11] Capital in this way spontaneously produces its premises: "In the completed bourgeois system, every economic relation presupposes every other in its bourgeois economic form, and everything posited is thus also a presupposition; this is the case with every organic system."[12]

But a "completed" economic system doesn't drop from the sky. A new system emerges initially based upon historic premises, those it inherits from the previous society rather than those it produces itself, and "its development to its totality consists precisely in subordinating all elements of society to itself, or in creating out of it the organs which it still lacks."[13] For capitalism to become an organic system, capital needed to alter the mode of production and to create a "specifically capitalist mode of production." As indicated in the Introduction to this book, once that capitalist process of production is "fully developed," capital produces the workers it needs, the presupposition of workers who look upon capital's requirements as common sense.[14]

However, what ensures the reproduction of the worker as wage laborer *before* capital has "posited the mode of production corresponding to it"?[15] Faced with workers who do *not* look upon the requirements of capitalist production as self-evident natural laws, workers who by education, tradition, and habit still consider the sale of their labor-power as unnatural, "the rising bourgeoisie needs the power of the state." Thus capital proceeded to subordinate all elements of society to itself through the coercive power of the state (for example, "grotesquely terroristic laws"), using this power to compel workers "into accepting the discipline necessary for the system of wage-labour."[16]

Accordingly, until the development of the specifically capitalist mode of production, the reproduction of capitalist relations of production required a specifically capitalist mode of *regulation*.[17] This mode of regulation was needed to prevent workers from extracting themselves from their dependence upon capital and entering a "diametrically opposed" relation—one where the producer "as owner of his own conditions of labour, employs that labour to enrich himself instead of the capitalist."[18]

In short, capitalism was not fully successful in "subordinating all elements of society to itself, or in creating out of it the organs which it still lacks" until it developed the specifically capitalist mode of production. Until the bourgeois system is "completed" as an organic system, elements are present in society that are alien to capitalist relations. Thus when we consider society at such a point, it is neither purely one system nor another. Rather, necessarily characteristic of the existing society is a *contested reproduction*—a struggle between differing productive relations, between "two diametrically opposed economic systems."

In *The Socialist Alternative*, I proposed that the same would be true for socialism. Until the associated producers develop their own specifically socialist mode of production, one that produces a working class that "by education, habit and tradition looks upon the requirements of that mode of production as self-evident natural laws," a socialist mode of regulation is required. Until socialism has developed upon its own foundations, the elements it inherits from the old society infect it, and the situation here too is one of "contested reproduction," a struggle between two opposed economic systems. In short, to ensure the reproduction of socialist relations of production under these conditions, a specific mode of regulation that subordinates the elements of the old society is essential.[19]

We need to pose the same questions with respect to Real Socialism. How was the system reproduced? Did it succeed in developing a specific mode of production which spontaneously produced its premise? Or did it require a specific mode of regulation to ensure its reproduction?

The Method of Political Economy

How do we get to the point of being able to explore such questions? For Marx, it was clear that the starting point must be a careful study of a real society. The concrete is "the point of departure for observation and conception." But empirical study in itself does not permit you to grasp the system as a totality; rather, you need the theorist's instrument, "the power of abstraction."[20] The method of inquiry, as Marx noted, "has to appropriate the material in detail, to analyse its different forms of development and to track down their inner connection." And that appropriation of the material in detail is a *precondition* for bringing "a science to the point at which it admits of a dialectical presentation."[21]

This dialectical presentation, then, is precisely what Marx called the "scientifically correct method." By starting from the study of the concrete, it is possible to distill simple principles that allow you to deduce elements in a sequence determined by the nature of their relations within the society in question.[22] Deduction allows you to understand the interconnections within the concrete whole and thus not to treat the elements as "independent, autonomous neighbours." To proceed from those simple conceptions to a conception of the whole "as a rich totality of many determinations and relations" was how Marx constructed the concept of the organic system. Through this method, he was able to demonstrate how the later logical developments in capitalism are latent in the simple concepts.

But the starting point must be that appropriation of the concrete in detail. That is what makes Janos Kornai's examination of Real Socialism such a useful scaffold. Beginning with his initial analysis of managerial behavior and the planning system in his native Hungary during the 1950s to his subsequent in-depth study of the "shortage economy" in general, to his later synthesis of the "immanent regularities of a socialist economy," Kornai's starting point was unquestionably the concrete characteristics of Soviet-type economies.

Making his analysis more than an empirical report, however, was Kornai's conscious attempt to imitate Marx's method. Thus, just as Marx pointed to "the completed bourgeois system [where] every economic relation presupposes every other in its bourgeois economic form," Kornai concluded that the characteristics of Real Socialism "exist not merely side by side and independently but in the closest of relationships with each other."[23] The phenomena, he noted, "all belong together and strengthen each other. This is no loose set of separate parts; the sum of the parts make up an integral whole."[24] In short, Real Socialism was definitely "a structure in which all the elements coexist simultaneously and support one another."[25]

For Kornai, Real Socialism was thus an organic system—a system whose "combination of main features forms an organic whole." It was a "coherent system," "a coherent whole" whose elements are "organically connected and reinforce each other." And, characteristic of that coherent totality is that "an affinity applies between the elements of it, so that they mutually complement and attract each other." Further, corresponding to Marx's description of the "becoming" of an organic system as consisting "precisely in subordinating all elements of society to itself, or in creating out of it the organs which it still lacks," Kornai argued that the process of becoming Real Socialism was one in which "specific forms and institutions grow *organically* within the system."[26]

That process is one in which "a natural selection of institutions and behavior patterns takes place, and ultimately enormously strengthens and greatly consolidates the inner coherence of the system." Indeed, once the key elements are present, the completion of the system tends to occur spontaneously: "The new structure proliferates with an elemental force, propagating itself and penetrating into every social relationship. Once the start of the process is imposed upon the society, it goes on in a spontaneous manner."[27] In this way, he argued, Real Socialism proceeded to produce its own premises—with the result that every economic relation presupposes every other in its "real socialist" economic form.

In short, Kornai attempted to "appropriate the material in detail, to analyse its different forms of development and to track down their inner connection." To represent Real Socialism as an organic system, he explicitly followed Marx's path of proceeding from simple concepts to a conception of the whole "as a rich totality of many determinations and relations." In Kornai's logical construction of Real Socialism, "a deductive train of thought . . . leads from a few main premises to an entire thought-network of conclusions."[28]

That combination of concrete study and a serious Marx-influenced attempt to grasp the inner structure and inherent tendencies of the system makes Kornai's work stand out among analyses of Real Socialism. However, as will be seen in this and succeeding chapters, I argue that he is *wrong* in his understanding of Real Socialism as an organic system. In order to reach this conclusion, he effectively assumed away "contested reproduction" and, in particular, the logic of capital.

Chronic Shortage

Start from the concrete: the characteristics of the Soviet Union and Eastern European countries following the Soviet model from roughly the 1950s through the 1980s. We begin with an obvious surface phenomenon—chronic shortage. Shortages facing consumers, shortages facing producers—in every aspect of life in Real Socialism, there was shortage. Indeed, responding to shortages was a way of life. The consumer went to the market and could not find what she wanted, so she had several choices: she could continue to search for that product, could postpone the decision to purchase until a later time, could join a queue, or could substitute another product for the originally desired one. All of these forced adjustments to disappointed purchasing intentions were part of life under shortages.[29]

So, too, was hoarding, when it was possible: "It is usual to say that every member of the household is recommended to carry a shopping bag in case he finds something worth buying. If he sees a queue, he should join it just to be safe—he can ask later what is being allocated."[30] Naturally, if you had more than what you needed of a particular item, there was always the possibility of trading it with someone who had what you wanted. Indeed, informal networks, personal contacts, favors for (and from) friends were means of survival within the context of shortages. In addition to the formal mechanisms, there was an informal principle of distribution: to each according to what his personal contacts can provide.[31]

The same patterns were true for enterprises and firms. As a seller in a seller's market, a characteristic of the shortage economy, the firm is in a favorable situation. However, as buyer, it also faces the problems of forced adjustment: it must wait, search, queue, or engage in forced substitution. It cannot easily postpone securing inputs, though, if it is to produce; thus "the firm, as buyer, tries to acquire as much input as possible in order that shortage should not hinder production."[32] This naturally intensifies shortages of those inputs and stimulates further hoarding. Of course, those stockpiled inputs may be traded with other firms for inputs in short supply; to ensure that enterprises could get the inputs they required in order to achieve their targets, their staffs included people (the *tolkachi* or "pushers") who could navigate well through such informal networks.

Was chronic shortage a matter of chance and contingency, of bad policies, or did it reflect something inherent in the nature of Real Socialism? According to Stalin, in his speech to the 16th Party Congress in 1930, under capitalism supply tends to outrun demand whereas in socialism demand tends to outrun supply: "In the USSR the growth of consumption (purchasing power) of the masses continually outstrips the growth of production and pushes it ahead, but under capitalism, on the other hand, the growth of consumption (purchasing power) of the masses never catches up with the growth of production and continually lags behind it, which condemns production to crises."[33]

Putting aside the question as to whether this was ever an accurate depiction, what was it about Real Socialism in the period under study that generated the phenomenon of chronic shortage? Was it the planners and "the plan" that created this situation? In his early work, *Anti-Equilibrium*, Kornai proposed that there were three immediate causes of the process of shortages or "suction": repressed inflation in trade of consumer goods, taut plans imposed upon enterprises, and the over-ambitious character of investment intentions. They all, though, could be reduced to *one* common source: "The reproduction of suction is ultimately related to impatient chasing of economic growth, the forcing of the acceleration of the growth rate."[34]

This was the same basic argument he had made over a decade earlier in his *Overcentralization in Economic Administration*: shortages were attributable to the unrealistic push for growth on the part of the central authorities and, via the ensuing pressure on those authorities, inevitably reinforce "centralized administrative forms of direction of the economy."[35] Accordingly, Kornai had concluded in the 1950s that shortages were not inherent but were the result of particular *policies*, policies that could be changed. Overcentralization, overly ambitious plans and shortages were all part of "a coherent, unified mechanism, which has its own inner logic and several tendencies and regularities peculiar to itself."[36] From this perspective, the remedy for the shortage economy was *decentralization*— decentralization of the economy and, in particular, decentralization of investment decisions. By moving away from centralized administrative direction of the economy, the self-reinforcing mechanism of centralization and shortages would be severed.

Of course, the begged question was why these patterns prevailed. The empirical test was soon available in the form of the decentralization carried out in Hungary. With the experience of those reforms, Kornai's position changed significantly—no, it *was not* those at the top who were the immediate cause of the shortage economy. "Even if central economic management were more moderate," he proposed in his major study on the economics of shortage, the drive for expansion and hunger for investment would still be present.[37]

THE PRINCIPLED MANAGER

Kornai's main explanation for the shortage economy became the expansion drive centered in individual enterprise managers. In particular, he emphasized the manager's "identification" with the job: "on average a firm's manager tries *to do his job properly.*" He "endeavors to secure subsistence, survival and viability of the unit put in his charge." He wants to guarantee a smooth working process. "He wishes to avoid confusion and disorder. If only for that reason, he strives for the largest possible security: procurement of more input and larger reserves." The manager further wants to "win his superiors' acknowledgement, avoid their anger, and to fulfill their expectations: not only their instructions but also their wishes."[38]

In short, Kornai proposed that shortages *really* were due to the principled behaviour and discipline of the manager. Criticizing those who continued to stress bureaucratic dependence and the emphasis upon growth by central authorities as the explanation of the quantity drive of firms, his earlier argument, Kornai now argued that the main explanation was the manager's identification with the job: "This general motivation is *sufficient in itself* to bring about the almost insatiable demand of the firm for inputs and, as we shall see later, an unquenchable expansion drive."[39]

With respect to investment itself, Kornai also explicitly retreated from his earlier view, stating now that the "growth policy of the economic leadership is a secondary explanatory factor."[40] "In a socialist economy," he proposed, "there is no firm or non-profit institution which does not want to invest." And again, Kornai emphasized the identification of the manager with his job as the central factor generating the expansion drive and investment hunger: "He is convinced that the activity of the unit under his charge is important. Therefore it has to grow." [41]

True, there were personal interests: "the leader's *power*, social prestige, and consequently his own importance grows together with the growth of his firm or nonprofit institution." However, material considerations were *secondary*. Even in their absence, the leader will "fight like a lion" for additional investment. The expansion drive, Kornai proposed, had become deeply rooted in thinking, "One *must* grow." This expansion drive was to be found at all levels of the economic hierarchy: "When it comes to the distribution of investment resources, each fights for more investment for *our* team, *our* firm, *our* ministry."[42]

And, it was a struggle on behalf of *our* workers. Given their identification with their own jobs and enterprises, managers also identified with their workers. Each manager *also* attempted to increase the level of wages of workers in his sphere. If, accordingly, workers attempted to increase their wages, they were not in battle against their immediate superiors: the managers "also fight for the correction of relative wages at all levels. The foreman wishes to remedy grievances on the shop floor, the firm's manager to remedy those of the firm, and the minister or his deputy wants to remedy those of the whole industry."[43]

Kornai thus proposed that there was a unique characteristic in these relations: management at all levels acts in wage negotiations with superior authorities *"as trade union officials and not as employers. . . .* Every manager tries to wring higher wages for his shop, section, etc., from his superior." This flows from the perspective of the manager: "The manager feels he is primarily responsible for solving the problems of the *part* of the system entrusted to him. He feels responsible not for the entire economy, but for a clearly specified part of it, and identifies himself with the latter."[44]

There's a rather significant problem, though, with this description of managerial motivation and behavior. It flies directly in the face of many other accounts of enterprise managers—beginning with that of Kornai himself!

Enterprise Managers as Agents

Consider the situation of the central economic authorities (the "planners"). In their central plan, they have broad goals for the growth of the economy over long periods of time (5 years, 15–20 years, etc.), which are specified generally (rates of growth, regional patterns, specific categories of production, etc.). And, by considering the input requirements for those goals, they attempt to identify potential obstacles and bottlenecks which could prevent realization of those plans. The shorter the time period, the more specific and targeted the goals.

Thus the annual plan specifies goals for the production of particular consumer goods and particular producer goods and assigns specific targets to enterprises. The planners try in this respect to coordinate the activity of enterprises as part of a single integrated national economic unit. They want the enterprises to meet those targets because fulfillment by each enterprise of its output target is necessary if other firms are to get their input requirements and if adequate and planned supplies of consumer goods are to be available. In other words, the success of the annual plan as a whole depends upon the success of the individual enterprises.

If we assume that the managers correspond to the description that Kornai offers, we would expect that these managers would recognize the interdependence that exists between their production targets and the success of the economy as a whole and thus they would act accordingly. The manager's identification with the job and his principled desire to do his job properly would be all that is necessary to ensure that the enterprise produced what the plan needed in order to ensure the coherence of the economy for a given time period.

But this is an assumption that the planners did not make. On the contrary, they assumed that the managers were motivated by material interest—that is, the managers acted as if they wanted to maximize their personal incomes in the present and the future. Indeed, Joseph Berliner commented at the time that "the predictability with which managers accommodate to a new bonus scheme may be compared to the fidelity with which a compass searches for the magnetic north. The manager himself is a wonderfully efficient computer program to maximize the value of any function fit into him that varies positively with income."[45] To encourage the managers to produce according to the plan, the planners provided bonuses (or "premia") for successful plan fulfillment.

And these bonuses were not a negligible part of the income of the managers. Berliner noted that though the bonus for Soviet enterprise managers in 1934 accounted for roughly 4 percent of their income (rising to 11 percent by 1940 in the context of attacks upon "equality-mongering"), this increased to 33 percent during the war but was driven down subsequently to 7.7 percent by 1960 as Khrushchev pushed to reduce income inequality. This de-emphasis upon bonuses was viewed as an error by those who replaced Khrushchev. According to Berliner, the average level of bonuses increased to 21.5 percent by 1966 and to 34.5 percent by 1970. Indeed, he noted one case of a well-managed enterprise (the Rostov agricultural machinery plant), where in 1966 bonuses of engineering and technical personnel represented 21.5 percent of their income and for directors and department heads, 40 to 60 percent of their income.[46]

Thus planners functioned on the premise that by specifying output targets (over the course of a year—for example, by month, quarter, etc.) and assigning a bonus for plan achievement, the managers would respond; this would ensure that enterprises would receive their inputs and that the stores would have the appropriate consumer goods. But how exactly was that output target specified? It *mattered*—because income-maximizing managers had discretion. In physical quantities or value terms (in order to aggregate different products, models, sizes, etc)? And, in the former case, how were those quantities specified?

The Soviet press demonstrated regularly how specification of targets mattered—ranging from the classic cartoon showing a frame with workers carrying one gigantic nail (with the heading, "the factory fulfills its plan") to the heavy chandeliers (denounced by Khrushchev) to the thick paper produced by the paper industry, incomplete buildings because construction enterprises were credited with more value added in the early stages of production than later, and the practice of "gold-plating" (where, for example, a clothing factory used material for a coat lining that cost twice as much as the cloth for the outside, thereby substantially increasing the value of the coats produced).[47]

These seemingly perverse phenomena were identified by Kornai in his classic study of light industry in Hungary in the 1950s. Giving an example of the characteristic of "turning 100 percent into a fetish," Kornai described a leather factory whose target was expressed in value. Since the value of work in progress could be factored in, the way to get a few extra percent in the last few days was to dump large quantities of raw hides into the soaking tanks. "The net value added," he noted, "is practically nil, but the material thrown into the dipper instantly assumes a value equal to 75 percent of that of finished leather for the purposes of reckoning total production."[48]

Every effort was made to ensure that plan fulfillment reached 100 percent. Thus managers became artists in devising methods for embellishing their results: "The smart economic administrators are past masters in the art of juggling with index numbers, and merely exploit the economic ambiguities and contradictions which are contained in the system of indices to which premium payments attach." On the same point, Kornai indicated that "it is not, in fact, possible to find a single director or other official concerned with plans who does not know how to conjure up an additional one or two percent, when really pushed to do so, in order to secure his premium—and this without any actual infringement of regulations."[49]

Closely associated to the 100 percent fetish was what Kornai described as "the periodic unevenness of production"—that is, the tendency for spurts of production and work in the last stages of the plan in order to make the quota. In the Soviet Union, the latter practice was known as "storming," and among its effects was a significant decline in the quality of output (a reason that the common wisdom was to try to purchase something produced in the first part of the month rather than after the middle of the month). There were constant complaints about the quality of output—for example, the vacuum cleaners that electrocuted you, which were mentioned in a Soviet newspaper of September 1985.[50] This problem was familiar and long-standing: the planning chairman in Czechoslovakia stated in 1951 that "storming is one of the most wasteful and costly ways of meeting the plan. It leads to unused equipment and manpower, to unused capacity, to waste of materials, to an increased number of rejects and to an uneconomical increase of wages by overtime pay."[51]

In short, the managers did everything possible to secure their bonuses. What could prevent this? A shortage of materials? The answer to that was to stockpile inputs and hoard materials. Difficulties in getting enough materials at key points? The answer was to produce it yourself. Or, do favors, bribe officials, or make alliances to make certain you got them. Shortages of workers on hand for the periods of storming? Stockpile and hoard workers.

But what happens, despite all these efforts, if the enterprise is still not close to its target? What happens if it is more like 10 percent away? What about the 100 percent fetish then? Kornai answered that what developed was "the psychology of losing hope." The managers would give up the struggle: "From a financial point of view (though not, of course, from a moral one) it is a matter of complete indifference to top management whether the degree to which they fulfill their indices amounts to 99 or 91 percent."[52]

Another reason for giving up the struggle in the short term was to save the potential output for the *next* plan period. Indeed, another category of problem identified by Kornai was the "conflict between today and tomorrow." Obviously the rush at the end of every month, that process of storming, could lead to shortages in the beginning of the next period—because of the exhaustion of input stocks and workers (producing, thus, the unevenness of production). A longer-term concern,

though, was the effect of this process upon the development of new manufacturing techniques, improved quality of products, maintenance of
equipment, training apprentices and skilled personnel. All of these affect
future performance; however, emphasis upon them could interfere with
meeting the *current* plan: "Timely work on maintenance may require the
stopping of machines, the continued working of which could assist very
materially with fulfillment of a monthly plan."[53]

Although Kornai did acknowledge that linking bonuses to plan fulfillment encouraged significant output increases, there was one aspect
of this focus upon material incentives that clearly affected the quality of
planning. Obviously, the probability of securing a bonus for plan fulfillment was greater, the lower the plan. "If the plan is loosely drawn up,"
he indicated, "this naturally eases the task of filling it, of obtaining the
premium in respect of it, and of winning moral approval. Top management of enterprises thus have a direct personal interest in being given a
loose plan to fulfill."

Accordingly, there was a systemic tendency to attempt to keep the
plan targets low—to "withhold information concerning the potentialities
and the reserves of their enterprises from the authorities."[54] The response
of enterprise managers to the demands from the top, according to the
Czechoslovakian economist and reformer Ota Šik, in 1968, was to adopt
"the most obvious mode of defense: they understated their potentialities and overstated their needs. . . . And there evolved a mechanism for
deception on a grand scale, of not showing one's hand, and this was the
only sphere in which people's initiative could really develop to the full."[55]

Alec Nove described the pattern in the following way:

> Information flows are *bound* to be affected, distorted, by the interests
> of the information-providers, who are in effect competitors for lim-
> ited resources. . . . But to expect unbiased information from those
> interested in the results to which the information is put is to live in
> cloud-cuckoo land.[56]

In other words, false information flowed upward. Here was the
dilemma: good planning depends on accurate information. But that was

not available because it was not in the economic interests of the managers to send accurate information upward. Šik commented that "the consequence is that Czechoslovak economy lost its last asset—objective information about needs, reserves and potentialities."[57]

Of course, the planners and officials in the ministries knew this was happening. They knew that firms were concealing information—in other words, that the quality of the information sent upward by enterprises was biased in favor of those enterprises. So they responded in a logical manner: they emphasized the necessity for taut plans in order to mobilize the hidden supplies of inputs; they argued that the enterprises were inventing "bogus difficulties." Enterprise managers and the planners thus were engaged in constant struggle over how tight or loose the plan would be. Given the orientation of the planners for growth, then, it was all so predictable that if the enterprise did demonstrate that it could produce very well, next year's plan would be higher. In other words, the results of any year's production would be incorporated into the next year's plan.

Naturally, that increase would make next year's plan more difficult to fulfill—and, more important, next year's bonuses more difficult to earn. So, the obvious behavior on the part of the enterprise manager was—do not overfulfill by too much. Maurice Dobb cited a Russian saying: "A wise director fulfills his planned 105 percent but never 125 percent."[58] Kornai had described the same phenomenon: "It is interesting to note that the chiefs of planning departments of enterprises become veritably frightened of the approach of the end of a quarter if they see that results will probably overshoot by too much."[59]

Naturally, the managers were able to find ways to keep output figures down as well as up—for example, to keep output from being counted as finished products. Kornai concluded that "in a word, present planning and incentive systems have evoked a spontaneous tendency, the effect of which is to induce managements of enterprises to loosen plans, to hide production potentials, and to hold back outstanding production achievements. This is highly dangerous and harmful."[60] In short, the clear picture that Kornai provided in the 1950s was that the behavior of the enterprise managers was contrary to the interests of society.

But not due to the shortcomings of *managers*! Rather, Kornai insisted, the problems were inherent in the existing system of economic administration and supervision of production results. These were necessary tendencies—but not necessary consequences of a planned economy *as such*. On the contrary, "They are necessary consequences of present methods of administering the economy, that is, of our present economic mechanism." Thus Kornai argued that it was the particular combination of instructions and incentives that generated these perverse results. Indeed, a chapter subhead told the story: "Some useful and harmful tendencies which result from the joint effects of plan instructions and incentives."

The problem was that managers were faced with a conflict between their economic interests and their sense of responsibility to the total economy; and "it is only human, if individual economic interest proves to be stronger."[61] The problem, Kornai stated, was the economic mechanism—the system of financial incentives was all wrong. The existing economic mechanism had to be changed—but it could not be changed as long as economic policy continued to insist upon "overambitious and unrealistic" targets.[62]

The problem, indeed, was signaled by the title of that 1959 book, *Overcentralization in Economic Administration*. That argument, though, was that overcentralization was the product of "excessively ambitious policies of industrialization," which themselves generated shortages (and thus a self-reinforcing process). If there were a lower pace of industrialization, then it would be possible for "an economic mechanism to develop in which enterprises have much more independence."[63]

So, what was his 1959 solution? Lower the targets for growth, decentralize, and unleash the enterprise. The enterprise, which was "the basic unit, the 'cell' of the economy," was given too many vertical instructions to carry out and had only minimal ability to engage in horizontal transactions with other enterprises.[64] And, even though his explanation for shortages in the 1970s (as we have seen) subsequently changed and stressed the expansion drive of the enterprise managers, *his solution remained essentially the same—give the enterprise managers more independence!*

It was not, after all, the particular behavior of those principled enterprise managers (who identified with their jobs and wanted to do good) that was the real source of the problem. Rather, the problem began at the top. Here we have Kornai's famous explanation: the expansion drive and investment hunger of the firms were only operative because the firms had "*soft budget constraints.*" The traditional socialist firm knew that, faced with losses, it would be "helped out somehow."[65] "Its permanent survival is guaranteed even in the case of a lasting financial deficit"; accordingly, only its resources constrain it.[66] The soft budget constraint, Kornai argued, uniquely characterizes the socialist firm and determines its expectations and particular behavior. The soft budget constraint, he declared, is a "sufficient cause" of investment hunger in the socialist economy.[67]

Once again, this pointed the responsibility for the reproduction of shortages directly *back* at the central authorities, for it is they who *soften* the budget constraints of the firms. Why? Kornai answered: "paternalism." Making an explicit analogy to the economic relationship between parent and child, he noted that "the central authorities take responsibility for the economic situation" and wish to "shape the course of economic life." Reinforcing paternalism from below on the part of the managers, too, is the simple fact that "paternalism means absolute protection and safety." Paternalism, Kornai concluded, "is the direct explanation for the softening of the budget constraint"—it entails "the almost-insatiable demand for labour and the tendency to hoard it, the almost-insatiable hunger for investment, and so on."[68]

So, although Kornai identified enterprise managers as the ones who were engaging directly in activities which had significant negative effects, the blame was to be found in the central authorities who created the incentives and the environment in which it was "only human" that the enterprise managers would act this way. Of course, the begged question (explored in the next chapter) is, *Why would the planners choose to follow policies that produced such negative effects?*

2—The Social Contract

A useful way to explore the interaction between planners and managers in Real Socialism is to consider it as a principal-agent problem.[1] In that framework, we assume the existence of a dominant party, a principal, who has a particular goal he wishes to achieve. And this principal must rely upon another party—the agent, who has his own goals, goals that differ from those of the principal. In other words, we begin by acknowledging that the interests of the principal and the agent are not identical. It is also presumed that the agent knows something the principal does not know (the problem of asymmetric information) and that it is difficult and costly for the principal to acquire that information. Accordingly, the principal-agent problem revolves around the mechanisms the principal uses to get the agent to act in accordance with the goal of the principal.

In the interaction we have described between planners and enterprise managers, it is customary to view the planner as the principal who attempts to induce the enterprise manager (the agent) to produce in accordance with the plan by providing material incentives in the form of bonuses for plan fulfillment. Certainly, as we see, the managers responded like that "wonderfully efficient computer program" to maximize their present and future income that Berliner described. Why, then, were the results so bad? Was this what the principal *wanted*?

Enterprise Managers as Principals

In the principal-agent model, it is assumed that the principal knows what the agent wants (that is, his utility function) and therefore creates the conditions that will produce the desired results. In this particular case, the premise is that the planner, though lacking the detailed knowledge necessary for planning, knows that the managers respond to material incentives and accordingly sets bonuses properly. So, if bonuses were primarily for short-run output plan fulfillment, we may presume that is because planners want to maximize output in the short run.

And yet it is clear that the planners were not happy with the results they were getting. All the stories about poor goods produced and perversities were attacks on the behavior of enterprise managers, attacks led and orchestrated by those at the top. It is no accident, for example, that the Soviet press was filled with such material. So what is the explanation if the planners were not getting the real results they wanted? Was it that they didn't know enough to introduce the proper incentive schemes?

By the time he wrote *The Socialist System*, Kornai had moved away from what he called naïve reformism to oppose socialism in any form. Now he explicitly rejected the argument that the principal-agent framework (which was a good fit for his own old argument) was appropriate to describe Real Socialism and that a reform of the economic mechanism could solve the problem. "Some observers and critics of the socialist economy," he commented, "tend to ask why a better information and incentive system is not introduced under socialism. They think society can be perceived as the realization of a gigantic 'principal-agent' model." From that perspective, the leaders must be assumed to have been stupid not to have found the right information and incentive scheme. But the leaders were *not* stupid—in fact, Kornai argued, the nature of the system was so coherent that it could not be altered by applying a few such ideas for reorganization.[2]

So, what was the problem? Before assuming that this was indeed a principal-agent problem—one to be settled by adopting the correct incentive scheme by planners—we need to ask if we have identified the actors correctly. *Maybe the managers knew the planners' goals better than the planners knew the managers' goals.* Maybe the managers were engaged in certain activities to induce the planners to select those mechanisms that were optimal for the *manager.*

In fact, this reversal is implicit in the concept of the soft budget constraint. It is the recognition by managers that the planners will not permit them to fail that leads the managers to act in particular ways. Though Kornai does not explore its implications, this is really the hidden subtext in Kornai's concept—that the managers' knowledge of planners' behavior permits the former to pursue (for whatever reason) their almost insatiable hunger to expand and that this creates the many problems generated by the resulting shortages. This inference can be supplemented by explicit examples of how actions initiated by enterprise managers generated significant dysfunctions in Real Socialism and created problems for the planners.

For example, Tamas Bauer argued that investment cycles, rather than being due to the unreasonable investment and expansion goals of those at the top, were generated from below. Enterprise managers had particular techniques for advancing their claims upon additional investment funds.[3] Given that the planners want to control the stock of investment projects in progress directly, he argued, "the claimants will find a way to break through it for hiding their claims (neglecting the necessary additional investments in the submitted plan proposals, etc.) or through underestimating investment costs." By starting an investment project with an artificially low amount of investment outlays in the first year, an enterprise could succeed in "hooking onto the plan" because the planners were primarily concerned at any given point with the annual investment outlays. The problem was that those at the top did not have good enough information to monitor and check this.

Thus, even if the planners wanted a feasible and harmonious investment plan, they would still be subject to strains from below. Bauer traces an investment cycle that begins with many new investment projects put in motion simultaneously. In the second phase, as the true extent of the projects under way emerges, growing investment outlays exceed significantly the planned investment; and a third phase occurs in which resulting shortages lead the central planners to put a check on

the approval of new investment projects and try to speed up completion of existing projects—moving ultimately to the postponement and
suspension of lower-priority investments and a lower approval of new
investments. Once the shortages abate, however, there is growing pressure to complete the postponed and suspended projects and to increase
the approval of proposals—and the cycle begins again.

Here, then, was Bauer's explanation for prolonged construction periods and delays in completions, the lower efficiency of investment, lower
growth rates, and a slower introduction of new technology. Was this pattern *inherent* in a planned economy? Not according to Bauer. Rather,
he argued that the pattern reflected the particular relations within the
economy: (a) the enterprise managers wanted investment funds because
it made plan fulfillment easier and a larger enterprise increased their
power status, and (b) enterprise managers knew that supervising bodies
would agree to support their investment claims if the managers accepted
the proposed quotas.

We come back, then, to Kornai's dismissal of the principal-agent framework as an explanation of the many perversities of the existing economic
mechanism. Kornai's point is that those at the top were not stupid. So,
were they *powerless*? Certainly, the managers were far from being passive
agents of the planners; rather, they constantly acted to take advantage of
"the ambiguities and blind spots of command planning to promote their
particular interests at the expense of overall economic development."[4]

Drawing upon his study of the literature of East European economists, Flaherty points out that enterprise managers went well beyond the
familiar defense mechanisms such as "the concealment of full production
capacity from the central authorities coupled with the deliberate inflation or distortion of production reports." Individual and uncoordinated
defense mechanisms, he argued, were "superseded by far more significant collective offensive strategies. These concerted responses originate
in the attempts of production subunits to procure organizational allies."[5]

Flaherty also proposed that lobbies and sectoral coalitions, which
became powers unto themselves, proceeded to usurp the authority of
the "nominally sovereign central agencies."[6] The result was that, in the
struggle for investment funds, the pattern of investment became "almost

entirely a function of sectoral dominance or the heavily skewed correlation of forces existing between the contenders in plan-bargaining."[7] Entrenched forces, particularly in heavy industry, trumped everything. And, the cost, some argued, was the absence of a coherent national industrial policy.

"In light of the destructive effects of sectoral dominance," Flaherty asked, "the obvious question becomes: why does the state not diagnose the obvious cause of these trends and take appropriate countermeasures to reassert its control against the monopolies?"[8] His answer is that it *tried*— by attempting to introduce additional regulations and planning indicators to resolve the problems; however, this simply triggered "redoubled efforts of lower-level production managers to evade the external scrutiny." The central authority was "increasingly incapacitated."[9]

Consider the apparent difficulty of shifting away from an extensive growth model based upon building new factories and filling them with a labor force drawn mainly from the countryside. Though this was the historic pattern of industrialization in Real Socialism, in the period under consideration the need to shift toward increasing productivity in existing production facilities was apparent. Ota Šik pointed out in Czechoslovakia that building new factories based upon resources siphoned off from existing enterprises came at the cost of modernizing existing plant and (because of the disproportionate focus upon heavy industry) satisfying consumer needs. The Czechoslovakian economy, he insisted in 1968, needed to "shift its emphasis in a relatively short period from long-term investment in heavy industry to the sectors that have suffered years of neglect."[10] Similarly, Kosygin received a major report in 1967 detailing serious problems in the Soviet economy, and in 1970 Gosplan issued a grim report critical of the direction of the economy and indicating that "all basic indicators will decelerate, deteriorate or stagnate."[11]

And, yet, nothing seemed to change. Speaking to the 27th Party Congress on February 25, 1986, Gorbachev stated that during the period of stagnation (the code word for the Brezhnev period) "we failed to apprehend the acute and urgent need for converting the economy to intensive methods of development." Rather, there had been continued development "largely on an extensive basis, with sights set on drawing additional labor and material resources into production." But why? Why did they not seem to be able to make the shift to intensive development?

Flaherty's sources offered one explanation. They argued that the inability to shift from the extensive development model to intensive development reflected in large part the power of the sectoral groups centered in heavy industry (both the enterprises and ministries). In Poland, the heavy industry and mining lobbies combined against reallocation of investment and thus continued to siphon off the bulk of new investments. Similarly, Brezhnev's attempt to move the Soviet economy slowly to an intensive growth pattern failed and demonstrated what was described as the center's "impotence before its subordinates" as sectoral coalitions succeeded in commandeering funds from weaker branches.[12]

CONSTRAINTS UPON THE PLANNERS

So, what was the basis of the "impotence" of those at the top? The power of the central authorities, Kornai stressed, is not absolute: "The 'politician' is not the external manipulator of a machine who can push buttons and turn levers at will." Rather, he "reacts with definite action to definite signals."[13] What determines those reactions?

In Kornai's macroeconomic model of the shortage economy, he introduced not only a "real sphere" that describes production, investment, consumption, etc. (standard aspects of an economic model), but also, significantly, a "control sphere" that represents the behavior of various decision makers.[14] Economic policy and decision patterns were modeled as endogenous to the system; and it is in this control sphere (through those definite reactions to definite signals) that the unique and specific characteristics of the socialist economy are generated.

At the core of this model is the question of *feedback*. Kornai's model describes not only the tendency for chronic shortage but also includes important feedback mechanisms that tend to reproduce a *"normal"* degree of shortage. Thus, where developments in the real sphere generate results that deviate from existing norms—the result of "habit, convention, tacit or legally supported social acceptance, or conformity"—the system generates signals that are fed back into the system via the control sphere. Very simply, deviations from the norms produce typical reactions, predictable behavior on the part of decision makers.[15]

This brings us, then, to the constraints upon the planners—that is, to their apparent powerlessness. What precisely occurred in that control sphere when norms were violated . . . and why? Take, for example, the normal rate of growth of real consumption per head. Kornai argued that this was a critical norm that central decision makers honored. Looking back over ten to fifteen years, he reported that many Hungarian planners viewed the "lower limit of tolerance" for this growth rate as 2 percent and the normal rate as 3–4 percent.[16] Deviations from this norm, he stressed, created a feedback mechanism: "If the growth of consumption remains below its normal rate, the scale of investment will be reduced so as to leave more of the national income for consumption."[17] But *why*?

What precisely produced the "control mechanism" that pushed the system back to the norm if it deviated? *A negative response by the underlying population*, according to Kornai. "Holding back increases in living standards, or their absolute reduction, and infringing the lower limit . . . sooner or later entails serious political and social consequences, tension and even shocks, which after a shorter or longer lag force a correction."[18]

Those at the top, he thus stressed, were limited. The barrier "depends on the actual socio-political situation, what level and growth rate of consumption the population is content to accept, and where dissatisfaction begins. And, if there is dissatisfaction, at what point it starts to endanger the stability of the system. It is a historical fact that unrest may be so great that it induces leaders to change economic policy."[19] In short, the growing consumption aspirations of the underlying population, he argued, were one element affecting the typical behavior of the central authorities; these aspirations could not be ignored.[20]

Closely associated with the desire of the population for rising income (along with the attendant constraint upon the planners) was their concern for stable prices. The potential for "irrationality," Kornai proposed, in this case was high. Although at one point prices might have been set appropriately (for example, reflecting old relative costs or permitting satisfaction of basic needs), relative costs and social preferences changed considerably over time. (Why, Kornai asked, should state subsidies for basic necessities, which encourage "overeating," be in the social interest?) The problem was that "rigidity and inertia prevent relative consumer prices from adjusting to new conditions."[21] Who, though, was rigid or conservative?

The people themselves. The issue, simply, was that movements in consumer prices were a "delicate political problem." The household budget constraint is hard; thus every price increase hits it hard, generating grumbling and protesting. "Precisely because a rather high degree of price stability is one of the greatest achievements of socialist economies, the population *expects* prices to remain unchanged; *stability in itself is of value to people*."[22] And so, this expectation on the part of the underlying population generated price rigidity. Any significant change in prices would have a major redistributive effect (as in the case, for example, of ending subsidized rents). "Any radical redistribution would upset public opinion. Those who gain by it may not even recognize their gain." This, Kornai explained, was the phenomenon of the "trap of price stability": "People get used to stability, and after a time they even expect the government to guarantee it. Any important price increase gives rise to unrest."[23]

It was, in short, the underlying population *itself* that was characterized by "rigidity and inertia." Not surprisingly, people were conservative in relation to measures that threatened their real incomes. Should the planners undertake an initiative in the direction of greater economic "rationality," they were directly pitted against habit and convention (that is, against popular acceptance of the existing norms).

The most significant norm, though, was the full employment norm. Kornai pointed out that "one of the basic historically important achievements of the socialist economy is full employment. Not only does it reach a high level of employment but, once having reached it, firmly guarantees it."[24] Unlike capitalism, with its buyers' market for labor in which market burdens (such as search, waiting, queuing and forced substitution) all fall upon the sellers, Kornai emphasized that socialism is marked by a sellers' market for labor—thus a high participation rate, absorption of potential reserves, and the elimination of chronic unemployment.

Accordingly, the "defenceless" feeling of workers in capitalism, which results from the threat of unemployment, is absent with the sellers' market in labor characteristic of socialism: "The person used to employment has no unemployed competitors in the market, nor is there any possible competition from a huge potential reserve army. *The behaviour of the group used to employment is characterized by guaranteed employment.*"[25]

So, was this a significant constraint upon the planners? To the extent that full employment was an expectation on the part of the population, would the violation of this norm produce "serious political and social consequences, tension and even shocks"? We need to understand more about the dimensions of this employment norm if we are to assume that it did indeed compel the planners to follow a particular course.

Job Rights

In 1975, David Granick argued that the right to a job in the Soviet Union involved far more than full employment at the macro level—it also functioned at the micro level. "It is considered impermissible, except in very rare circumstances," he indicated, "to dismiss workers on any grounds other than those of gross incompetence or continued violation of factory discipline." In short, "workers have had virtually complete job security. More than anything else, it is this feature which has given content in the mind of the ordinary worker to the slogan of a workers' state."[26]

The "political unacceptability of dismissals" thus gave workers real security; they were "protected, not only against the reality of unemployment, but also against the need to change either occupation or place of work under the threat of unemployment."[27] This characteristic, which Granick called the "micro-economic full employment" constraint (but which he would later call "job rights"), meant that workers were "virtually immune from pressure to undergo job changes which they personally regard, for whatever reason, as reducing their individual welfare."

Yet what was positive for workers registered as essentially negative for Kornai. His discussion of the employment norm clearly demonstrates (if there were ever any doubt) that his concept of rationality reflected all along the perspective of the enterprise manager (the "cell" of the economy). In the absence of external slack in the labor market, that is, in this sellers' market for labor, Kornai argued, the buyer (the manager) bears the costs of search, information collection, waiting, etc.[28] Further, under these conditions of shortage, firms are compelled to hoard and reserve labor for the future. From this perspective alone, "adjustment" of the employment norm was justified—a little slack in the labor market (a reserve army of the unemployed) would be rational.

The greater problem for Kornai, though, was "internal slack"— "unemployment on the job." Kornai proposed that "the more frequent and intensive the labor shortage, the greater will be the internal slack, namely the unemployment on the job." Why? Because "chronic and intensive labour shortage loosens workshop discipline, deteriorates work quality, lessens workers' diligence." He noted that "most people . . . do their work reasonably well without external pressure to do so. And the more they understand the social importance of their work, the truer is this statement." But *the factors operating in favour of discipline, diligence, and care are counteracted by chronic labour shortage. The worker's absolute security, the unconditional guarantee of employment, encourages irresponsibility in anyone susceptible to it.*"[29]

And what could the managers do about this? Managers (including foremen) were restricted in imposing discipline; they were forced by the sellers' market "to be indulgent." The causal chain: the greater the intensity of labor shortage, the more frequently workers unexpectedly leave jobs to take others (with the positions remaining unfilled). "Alternatively, they may not leave, but simply be absent without justification, or they come to work, but instead of working properly just waste time."[30] Few things, clearly, were worse in Kornai's eyes than the typical behavior of workers in this shortage economy.

Obviously, functioning in this sellers' market for labor was a problem for enterprise managers. The other side, of course, is that the shortage economy and the full employment norm provided immediate benefits for workers. But what about the central economic authorities, the planners? Did Kornai explain that the full employment norm (like the other norms) constrained the planners, compelling the decisions that reproduced the shortage economy? In fact, he said surprisingly little about this. As Granick commented about Kornai's *Anti-Equilibrium*, "There is nothing in his treatment either of the history or of the logic of suction to suggest any role at all for the job-maintenance constraint which I consider fundamental."[31] And once Kornai shifted his explanation of shortages to stress the insatiable investment hunger of managers, any direct link in his analysis between the full employment norm and planners' behavior became even more obscure.

Nevertheless, given that "in Kornai's model little or nothing is invested without the approval of the Center," adaptation of the plan to the investment hunger of the managers is "a necessary condition for the investment strains that lead to labor shortage." Since "it is only the yielding by the Center to requests that causes labor demand for future periods to be unconstrained," Kornai's theory begged that critical question—why did the center agree? [32]

To try to answer this question, we need to know more about this employment norm. It appears to have had (at least) three relevant aspects: (a) economic pressures that create the sellers' market for labor, thereby ensuring a high probability that jobs are available for everyone; (b) political and legal pressures to place people in jobs; and (c) political and legal pressures to protect people from losing their jobs or being compelled to change them in some way. Obviously, these are related; however, if we consider only the first of these (full employment), we are likely to misunderstand their underlying basis.

Let us begin with the last of these—job rights, "the worker's *absolute* security," the de facto right of the individual worker to his existing job. This job right was supported explicitly in the labor legislation introduced in the post-Stalin period. Article 17 of the Fundamental Labor Legislation of the USSR (1971), for example, restricted the basis for dismissal of a worker to specific grounds and noted that even these grounds were valid only "if it is impossible to transfer the employee concerned to another job with his consent."[33]

In theory, a worker could be dismissed for violating labor discipline (for example, absenteeism and drunkenness on the job), for being unwilling or unable to perform their existing tasks, and for redundancy (i.e., because they were unneeded). In practice, however, it was not so easy. The first line of defense of the worker was the elected workplace trade union committee. Before any dismissal, that committee had to agree; and this had to occur at a full meeting, would require a two-thirds quorum and an absolute majority voting for dismissal.[34] And that decision, if it favored the worker, could not be overturned (a power that Granick described as "truly striking" because of the usual principle in Real Socialism whereby "a hierarchically higher body can always overturn the decision of a lower one.")

Assuming the trade union committee supported dismissal, however, the worker could always turn to the courts. Lewin indicates that "in 1965, in 60% of the cases brought before them, tribunals had ordered the reinstatement of sacked workers"—with back pay, which meant "serious costs" for the government.[35]

Workers were also protected from job changes and transfers to other work—even in clear cases where they were made redundant by technological changes and reorganization. In such cases, most workers whose job had disappeared were retrained in the same enterprise. If they refused, however, they again had resort to the trade union for protection and to the courts (and they were even more successful here). All this happened in a context where there was a constant effort to find jobs for new entrants to the labor market—for example, pressure on enterprises to hire young people. The existence of unemployment in specific areas brought with it as well pressure by local party committees that all local enterprises add to their workforce. This was a practice supported by Article 9 of the Labor Legislation, which stated that "unfounded refusal to grant a job is prohibited by law."[36]

The protection that individual workers had for their jobs from trade unions and the legal systems was real. However, as Lewin notes about the USSR, "employees possessed a more effective weapon than resort to the courts: they could defend their interests by changing jobs."[37] In short, the existence of suction and the shortage economy meant that workers could ensure their rights within the workplace (including the right to a workday with a pace that was decidedly not intense—another norm). In this sellers' market for labor, workers were able to move freely—and they took advantage of that opportunity. Thirty percent of the Soviet industrial manual labor force left its existing enterprise in a given year—despite the measures that enterprise managers developed to retain their workers, such as upward job classification, provision of housing, childcare, etc.[38]

How important, then, was this combination of job rights and the shortage economy for understanding Real Socialism? Granick argued that the condition of "Job-Rights-Overfull-Employment" (JROE) took "precedence over most other objectives of central planners in the Soviet Union." One might see it, he proposed, as a key goal of central planners that "must be satisfied fully before other objectives are pursued." The alternative argument, he acknowledged, is that JROE was a *constraint* facing central planners, imposed upon them "against their will."[39]

Which was it? Granick insisted that ensuring job rights was the preferred policy of the Soviet leaders—whether it was because they themselves preferred it or because they "believe that the political reactions of the Soviet population to violations ... would be so severe."[40] The latter was the same point he had made earlier about Hungarian reforms: "meddling with this fundamental right of Hungarian workers would raise in the sharpest form the issue of the abandonment of socialism: in the minds both of the population of Hungary and of leaders in the other CMEA countries."[41] In any event, he argued that the economic result would be the same whether the typical behavior of planners occurred because these norms were their own or because failure to honor them would start "to endanger the stability of the system."

Given that maintenance of these norms, however, was subsequently abandoned by those at the top, it is important to ascertain if planners and workers had identical goals. Consider, for example, the distinction between full employment (the right to a job in general) and job rights (the right to a particular job—what Granick called the micro-economic full employment constraint). Speaking to a group of workers, Janos Kadar, prime minister of Hungary, argued that "full employment is our system's achievement." However, "at the same time the rational regrouping of labor is unavoidable. The development and expansion of economical production, the contraction and finally cessation of uneconomical production require the appropriate regrouping of labor."

What did this reveal? Ed Hewitt's interpretation was that by 1981 the Hungarian party and government leaders were at the point that "they define full employment as the guaranteed right to a job, but not to a particular job, nor to a particular way of doing that job." And that meant that "in the next few years they shall try to convince the population" of the need to regroup workers. Here were "two very formidable stumbling blocks to further economic reform in Hungary. The population is convinced that a fair income distribution is a flat one, and they are convinced that the party's guarantee of a job means that each person can keep the job he or she has right now."[42] Those at the top, in short, were clearly constrained by what workers considered their entitlement.

But this brings us to what some would consider a paradox of Real Socialism. Consider the phenomenon of job rights—the package that included security of employment, a relatively leisurely pace of work, and the availability of alternative jobs because of full employment. These were characteristics that would be recognized as great achievements as the results of workers' struggles in capitalism. *But they were not achievements of workers in Real Socialism—the working class and working-class organizations were not strong enough to ensure them and to protect them.*

Here was the paradox of the situation of workers in the Soviet Union as summarized by Linda J. Cook:

> Its working class was until recently politically quiescent and organizationally weak, denied rights to form independent trade unions, to organize political parties, indeed to engage in effective or meaningful political participation. Yet Soviet workers seem to have gotten from post-war regimes major policy goals—full and secure employment, rising real incomes, and socialized human services—which have remained inaccessible to the best organized labor organizations in the industrialized world. How can we explain this paradox?[43]

What was the organizational representation of workers? As we have seen, the official trade unions protected the rights of individual workers; however, their leaders were nominated from above and their principal function was to serve as a transmission belt to mobilize workers in support of state goals. Article 96 of the Fundamental Labor Legislation noted that the trade union organizations participated in the drawing up of state economic development plans (at the top) and "they enlist the factory workers and office employees in the management of production; they organize socialist emulation, mass-scale participation in promoting new ideas in technology, and help to promote production and labor discipline."[44]

However, not a word about workers' *power* within the workplace—not unless (as Article 97 notes) their right to take part in discussions and to "submit proposals on improving the work of enterprises, institutions and organizations" is interpreted as power. And not unless it is seen as an achievement of workers that "the officials of enterprises, institutions, organizations must promptly consider proposals and criticism made by the factory workers and office employees, and inform them regarding the steps taken on these matters."[45] In other words, the company will be happy to receive suggestions from workers—and the company will decide which ones, if any, it will follow.

No power within the workplace to direct the process of production, no ability for workers to transform themselves in the course of transforming things, but protection of individual job rights (especially against initiatives of enterprise managers). The picture is one of an atomized yet secure workforce, a situation "where the atomized, alienated worker, deprived of any and all means of exerting collective defence of her or his interests within production and society at large, could and did assert substantial individual control over the organization and execution of work." And its result was "slow work, defence of inefficient work organization, toleration, if not exacerbation of disruptions to the work regime, and a general disregard for quality."[46] Was this result what workers wanted? Was it what planners wanted?

THE NATURE OF THE SOCIAL CONTRACT

According to Lewin, the witty remark, "You pretend to pay us and we pretend to work," contained "a grain of truth—i.e., the existence of a tacit social contract, never signed or ratified, whereby the relevant parties arrived at an understanding about running a low-intensity, low-productivity economy."[47] Yet the social contract identified above went well beyond this; it involved not only job rights, but also rising income, subsidized necessities, and relative egalitarianism—all in return for acceptance of the power of the state and party and restrictions on any power from below.[48]

Did this contract deliver to workers what they really wanted or was it the best they could get under the circumstances? Cook proposed that "what the Soviet state delivered was precisely what its society most valued, that is, that party and people shared a conception of distributive and social justice that gave central place to material welfare and egalitarianism."[49]

Given the absence of a mechanism by which workers could express what they wanted, however, how could we know this? Certainly, it would be important to know what happened to workers who concluded that the terms of the contract were just not good enough. Flaherty noted, for example, reprisals against individual Soviet workers who challenged conditions in their workplaces and commented: "The corporatist *status quo* of the Brezhnevian social contract is the balance between the most that the dominant class will concede and the best that the subaltern class can expect, given the 'mercilessness of life' in a modern industrial society."[50]

In short, though this social contract provided definite benefits for workers, it should not be assumed that its conditions were those negotiated by workers or indeed their choice. "There was a system of mutual obligations," Boris Kagarlitsky explained:

> We use the term "obligatory social contract" or asymmetrical social contract, meaning that the population was forced into this social contract. The social contract was definitely not free. On the other hand, if you lived in the country you understood that, though the population was forced into this contract, it was accepted, not just because there was no other way, but because people liked certain aspects of the contract.[51]

Who, then, chose this contract and why? To understand Real Socialism, we need to explore the particular relationship between workers and the group we have been calling the planners.

Consider the course of our discussion of Real Socialism. We began with a "real fact," the real concrete. The omnipresence of the phenomenon of shortages was our point of departure, and we traced the apparent source of shortages to the relation of planners and enterprise managers. Further analysis, however, led to the conclusion that the inner connection that generated these phenomena was to be found in the relationship between planners and workers—a relationship crystallized in the simple concept of the social contract. With this concept, we can try to retrace our steps to develop an understanding of Real Socialism as a whole.

We should note immediately, though, two silences related to the concept of the social contract. One concerns the place of the enterprise managers. After all we have said about them in this chapter, where do they fit in this social contract?

The second silence concerns the key link between human development and practice. Where in this discussion of the social contract is there a focus upon the full development of human beings, a stress upon revolutionary practice, the emphasis upon the development of people through their activity in the sphere of production and in every aspect of their lives, the development of socialist human beings?

These silences are not accidental. In this concept of a social contract between planner and worker or, rather, between vanguard and worker, we can see the characteristics of the dominant relation of production in Real Socialism. This apparent social contract permits the reproduction of that relation, which we will call the *vanguard relation of production*.

3—The Nature and Reproduction of Vanguard Relations of Production

Beginnings are critical—especially when you are attempting to understand a complex combination of elements. When you start an examination of Real Socialism by focusing upon juridical property rights (state ownership of the means of production) and a coordinating mechanism (central planning), inevitably the centrality of the relations of production characteristic of Real Socialism is displaced. What are the social relations within which production, distribution, and consumption take place? Whose goals dominate production? Who rules within the workplace? What are the relations among producers? We always need to keep in mind that all production occurs within and through a particular set of social relations.

So, where to begin? Choice of a starting point in a logical construction cannot be arbitrary; rather, it should flow from an analysis of the specific concrete. Accordingly, after concluding our consideration of Real Socialism by stressing the importance of the particular social contract between "planners" and workers, we begin with what we designated in the last chapter as the vanguard relation of production. If we begin here, though, doesn't this imply that the state ownership and central planning we observe in Real Socialism should be understood as the *vanguard* form of state ownership and the *vanguard* form of central planning? Obviously. In a dialectical construction, all the later moments are implicit in the starting point.

However, we need to take care about such an inference: it presumes that vanguard relations of production coincide precisely with Real Socialism. Yet, by excluding the managers from the social contract, we already have indicated that Real Socialism is *not* composed only of vanguard relations of production. More than one relation existed. As we will see, there was a process of contested reproduction, and the phenomena from the 1950s through the 1980s described in the previous chapters in many respects result from this contestation. Further, we need to consider whether the social contract described there represents vanguard relations as such or whether it was one particular mode of regulation for their reproduction that existed in a given period.

The Vanguard Party

After years of experiencing and studying Real Socialism, Kornai chose to begin his ultimate work on it with the Communist Party. Indeed, he indicated at the outset of *The Socialist System* that "the sole criterion" he used for designating a country as socialist, was the undivided power of a communist party.[1] By definition for Kornai, socialism "comes into existence only when and where the Communist Party is in power."[2] Accordingly, rule by the Communist Party is "necessary and sufficient for the system to emerge and consolidate."[3]

> The Communist Party must gain undivided possession of political power for the process to get under way. This historical configuration bears the "genetic program" that transmits the main characteristics of the system to every cell within it. This is the seed of the new society from which the whole organism grows.[4]

In short, for Kornai the organic system, Real Socialism, is latent in the Communist Party. "This 'genetic program' fashions society in its own image; it creates a coherent system whose various elements connect, and assume and reinforce each other."[5] State ownership, the state-party relation, central planning—these are just some of the elements that for Kornai flow from this premise through a deductive train of thought. "The prime factor that brings the other system-specific phenomena about," he argued, "is the undivided power of the Communist Party imbued with its specific ideology."[6]

As indicated earlier, we part company very significantly with Kornai's analysis and conclusions. However, both his starting point and his attempt to deduce "system-specific phenomena" from this logical premise lead in the right direction. So, we begin with one side of vanguard relations, the vanguard party. In doing so, though, our initial focus is upon the *logic* of the vanguard—that is, the vanguard party in its "purity" rather than how it may have been infected in the course of its interaction with other elements (both contingent and inherent).

Let us begin, then, by proposing three tenets or doctrines of the vanguard party:

1. *The goal of system change*: an absolute commitment to replacing capitalism with socialism and to building a communist society (which has as its premise the appropriate development of productive forces).

2. *The need for a political instrument*: to achieve this goal requires a political party with the mission and responsibility of organizing, guiding, and orienting the working class, all working people, and social organizations.

3. *The necessary character of the vanguard party*: the struggle to defeat the enemies of the working class requires a disciplined, centralized, and united revolutionary party—*our* party.

Consider these three points. The goal of system change distinguishes the concept of the vanguard party from a body of self-interested bureaucrats or would-be capitalists. It begins from a clear rejection of capitalism as a system and the belief in the necessity of socialism. Given that essential goal, the question is, what is to be done? Characteristic for the supporters of the vanguard party is the conviction that the achievement of this goal will not happen spontaneously and, accordingly, requires leadership. This orchestra, in short, needs a conductor: "The interconnection and unity of the process is necessarily represented in a governing will."[7] And that governing will must be the party. As Stalin put it, "the Party must stand at the head of the working class."[8]

This self-conception of the party as the necessary conductor on the road to socialism and communism is one that brings with it responsibility and duties—the goal is "the only thing that counts, and no one is more convinced of this than the conductor himself."[9] To fail to lead would be to betray the working class. Describing the self-conception of the role of the Communist party in Real Socialism, Kornai wrote: "The working class does not exercise power directly; it is represented by the party. The party is the vanguard of the working class and so ultimately of the whole of society. As such it is destined to lead society."[10]

The party, in short, takes on the role of educator to pupil, leader to the led, and conductor to the conducted. Delivering its "banked knowledge" in the form of "Marxism-Leninism," the party is the teacher, the ideological mentor of the people, and their compass. Of course, to avoid confusion in the working class and the whole of society, any differences internal to the party must be hidden—there can only be one accepted understanding of Marxism-Leninism, one teacher, one conductor to guide the process. Socialism in this perspective is a gift to those below by the only ones above who know how to create socialism.[11]

But who accepts this responsibility of leading society? Those who combine the commitment to building socialism, the recognition of the need for party leadership, and the acceptance of the importance of unity are the logical members of the party. "Many members of the apparatus," Kornai acknowledged, "are people guided by noble purposes who work long, hard hours in the firm belief that in doing so they serve the cause of their party and of the people, the common good and the interests of mankind."[12] He returned to this point when describing the motivations of members of the state bureaucracy in Real Socialism: heading Kornai's list of the complex combination of motives (which include an interest in power, prestige, and material benefit) is "political and moral conviction" based upon "belief in the party's ideas, agreement with the official ideology, and enthusiasm for the plan's objectives."[13]

This political and moral conviction that leads party members to work "long, hard hours" to build socialism does not drop from the sky. The first principle of vanguard party recruitment is to attract those people who have demonstrated, through their (honest or simulated) behavior in their workplaces and communities, that they are good candidates and will accept the party's responsibilities and its norms.

Once in the party, these recruits logically should be exemplary and positive examples for all others within society. Thus they are expected to be self-sacrificing, to set an example of the communist attitude toward work, to respect, protect, and care for socialist property and to struggle to implement the party's positions even after having argued and voted against them.[14] Further duties stress the importance of placing social interests above personal interests, setting an example of sensitivity and human solidarity, strengthening and broadening the relations between the party and the masses, trying to win the best workers and other citizens over to revolutionary activism and holding high the principles of internationalist unity and cooperation. *How could this not attract the best, the most idealistic young people within the society?*

However, not everyone committed to the goal of building the socialist society and prepared to be self-sacrificing would qualify as a good party member. The member was expected to study deeply the party ideology, work to implement party decisions, accept the process of criticism and self-criticism, and be willing to subject oneself to party discipline. Not everyone is prepared to do that. Further, even if you are, the decision is not yours alone. To be accepted as a party member, a candidate has to be accepted not only by a local unit but also by the next higher body of the party. The principle that those who are above decide, in short, is embodied within the very structure of the vanguard party. And it is the continual presence of that hierarchical principle that characterizes the party and shapes individual behavior from the time of initial entry.

There is a particular logic to this. Since the struggle to build social-ism requires unity and discipline within the party, the internal structures must reflect those obligations. For this purpose, the party relies upon "democratic centralism"—which may be defined as the greatest possible democracy in arriving at decisions and the greatest possible centralism and discipline in executing those decisions. Described as such, demo-cratic centralism is only common sense.

That democracy, however, is episodic—limited in general to party congresses and other collective decision-making occasions. Discipline and centralism, in contrast, are part of daily life and responsibilities for party members. Illustrating the primacy of the latter, consider the very first point in "the basic principle of democratic centralism" of the Communist Party of China:

> (1) The individual Party member is subordinate to a Party organization, the minority is subordinate to the majority, the lower level organization is subordinate to the higher level, each organization and all members of the whole Party are subordinate to the Party's National Congress and the Central Committee.[15]

Thus, a top-down process that, Kornai commented, in practice *inverts* the underlying concept of democratic centralism. Rather than a process of organization from below, in practice what exists is a "bureau-cratic hierarchy that encompasses the whole of the party: instructions passed down from above must be carried out by the subordinates."[16] Structure and ideology interpenetrate because "the code of moral imper-atives" for party members in the official ideology emphasizes discipline: "The prevailing political line must be followed, the decisions endorsed, and the commands of superiors obeyed without hesitation."[17]

There is, however, another very important aspect of this inversion of a bottom-up process. And that is the tendency for the top to select the bottom—that is, the tendency for those at the top of the hierarchy to appoint as subordinates those people they feel can be trusted to carry out their policies. We have here the concept of the *nomenklatura*, the list of those who can be trusted. The inverted circuit is complete when those who have been appointed from above (and therefore owe their loyalty upward rather than to those below them) proceed to choose the leaders of the party and vote upon policies.

While such a structure can be efficient in achieving specified party objectives, how could it not affect the nature of party members produced as joint products of these processes? Recall the principle of the "key link" of human development and practice—that simultaneous changing of circumstances and human activity or self-change that Marx called "revolutionary practice." What kinds of people are produced within these hierarchical relations? They are people who do not want to be viewed as deviating from party norms and decisions, as engaging in individualistic behavior and thereby placing themselves "above the party"; they are people who discipline themselves accordingly.

Describing the long-term effect upon members of the bureaucratic structure of such patterns, Kornai wrote:

> It is unwise to criticize upward, come out with unusual ideas, or take initiatives. It does not pay to think for oneself or take risks on one's own. . . . The character-forming and training effect, and the selection criteria of bureaucratic control, reinforce each other: servility and a heads-down mentality prevail.[18]

Similarly, the Polish economists Brus and Laski described the paralysis of initiative, boldness, and innovativeness within the bureaucracy: "A major factor strengthening these attitudes is the Nomenklatura system of selection to positions of responsibility, which promotes the obedient followers of the party line in preference to the independent, daring, and imaginative."[19] While both references relate to the character of behavior within the state bureaucracy, it is essential to understand that the "genetic program" is already present in the vanguard party.

Indeed, the reproduction of the vanguard party is ensured by the fact that the best and most idealistic within the society are recruited and that their formation leads them to accept the principle that the party must direct from above and is always right. There is an interesting parallel described by Marx in volume 3 of *Capital* in which he noted that the ability of an individual man without wealth to rise to become a capitalist "actually reinforces the rule of capital itself." He continued:

> The way that the Catholic Church of the Middle Ages built its hierar-
> chy out of the best brains in the nation, without regard to status, birth
> or wealth, was likewise a major means of reinforcing the rule of the
> priests and suppressing the laity. The more a dominant class is able to
> absorb the best people from the dominated classes, the more solid and
> dangerous is its rule.[20]

Of course, describing the logic of the vanguard does not at all mean that we are ignoring the existence of privilege or self-interest on the part of individual members of the vanguard—any more than Marx ignored "the desire for enjoyment" on the part of capitalists. One could certainly look at individual capitalists and stress their luxury consumption and make that the focus. That, however, was not central to Marx's analysis. He stressed the capitalist as the bearer of the logic of capital rather than the capitalist as private consumer: "Insofar as he is capital personified, his motivating force is not the acquisition and enjoyment of use-value" but the growth of capital. While "two souls" dwelt within the breast of the capitalist, it was "only as a personification of capital" that he drove "the human race to produce for production's sake" and spurred on "the development of society's productive forces."[21] In the same way, individual members of the vanguard are stressed here only as a personification of the vanguard—that is, as the bearers of the logic of the vanguard. In short, our discussion focuses upon the logic of the vanguard as it attempts to spur on "the development of society's productive forces."[22]

THE WORKING CLASS UNDER VANGUARD RULE

Of course, we have been considering only one side of the vanguard relation. Clearly, a premise of the relation described at this point is that the working class accepts the leadership of the vanguard party as well as its own subordinated role within the social contract. The lack of power to make decisions within the workplace, the atomization and inability to organize collectively within the workplace or within society in general—all this reflects the vanguard's belief that the march to socialism requires a directing authority that is the vanguard party itself. Thus an essential part of that social contract is that workers are contained in official trade unions, official sport societies, official women's and peace movements, etc., and that any efforts to create independent forms of organization are viewed as heresies and threats to the entire relation.

As discussed in the last chapter, the working class accepts all this insofar as it is able to achieve its *own* goals in the social contract. An essential part of that contract is protection and security from unemployment and the maintenance of their job rights (which keeps the length and intensity of the workday low). Added to job rights, too, was the expectation of rising income over time, subsidized necessities, and relative egalitarianism. Thus, as we have seen, the working class yields control over its labor power in return for a package that is far better than that it could expect to receive within capitalism.

Yet that acceptance is conditional—it is conditional upon the vanguard delivering on its side of the contract. Central decision makers, we saw, *worried* about this—for example, worried about not achieving the norms for the growth of consumption. They worried about "serious political and social consequences," about the emergence of dissatisfaction and at what point dissatisfaction "starts to endanger the stability of the system."[23] To paraphrase Lenin (in his comments about the peasants and the need for NEP in the Soviet Union in the 1920s), they worried that within the social contract the working class allows the vanguard party credit but there may come a point when the working class "will demand cash."

Of course, when discontent emerges, the party can use "the whole arsenal of education and modern political propaganda" to attempt to elicit support for its policies. "But to augment the arsenal and give special emphasis to the words of enlightenment there is repression."[24] If repression rather than accommodation, however, is a general response to the reaction to its own failure to meet its side of the contract, this suggests a unilateral abandonment of that social contract by the vanguard. That is certainly a possibility. Let us, however, explore what logically flows from the attempt to *satisfy* the terms of this contract.

THE STATE AND STATE OWNERSHIP

Dialectical reasoning requires us always to ask—what is *implicit* in the categories we have considered? What flows from the concept of the vanguard party? What must the vanguard party do to build socialism? Firstly, since the party has the responsibility to lead society, it must have the *power* to do so. It must control the state—and there is no logical basis for sharing this power with other parties or for relinquishing it voluntarily. Further, given its opposition to capitalist exploitation, the party must use that power "as soon as politically practicable, to organize society on a basis of public instead of private ownership."[25] So Kornai argued, state ownership of the means of production in the socialist system flows from this political structure:

> The primary attribute of the socialist system is that a Marxist-Leninist party exercises undivided power. Now, a further characteristic can be added: the party is committed to eliminating private property, and with its undivided power and interpenetration with the state, it manages sooner or later to put that program into practice, or at least come near to doing so.[26]

But this involves more than a transfer of juridical ownership to the state. *Also* transmitted to the state by this particular genetic program is the hierarchical pattern characteristic of the party. State ownership here occurs within a particular kind of state, one that reflects the "hierarchy that encompasses the whole of the party: instructions passed down from above must be carried out by the subordinates." So, to be effective, those at the top of this state must ensure that the right people are there to receive instructions; accordingly, "superior individuals ... are appointed over the subordinates' heads instead of being elected by them."[27] We see here the logical necessity for the nomenklatura, that list of those who have demonstrated their competence and loyalty.

Logically, too, the vanguard party must monitor the process by which its decisions are executed. Noting the extent to which major personnel decisions and decisions on critical questions were made by party bodies, Kornai commented that the "Communist Party considers itself responsible for everything and does not allow the organizations of state and those working in the state apparatus any autonomy at all. In fact, the existence of the 'party-state' and the blending of the political and administrative functions is one of the main characteristics of the system."[28]

By selecting the vanguard party as his starting point, Kornai made a significant conscious break with arguments that view state ownership of the means of production as the core of Real Socialism. Specifically, he insisted that "it is not the property form—state ownership—that erects the political structure of classical socialism over itself. Quite the reverse: the given political structure brings about the property form it deems desirable."[29] The pattern of property rights is thus logically a result rather than a premise. Whereas it is possible to deduce state ownership from the power and ideology of the vanguard party, we could not do the reverse. State ownership in itself, in short, is not a sufficient condition for Real Socialism; it does not imply the particular ideology, internal structure, and dominance of the vanguard party.

We immediately understand, then, Real Socialism as permeated by the character of the vanguard party. Within vanguard relations, state ownership of the means of production exists within a hierarchical structure. Thus it is not state ownership *in general*; rather, there is state ownership in its vanguard form. Won't this, then, be true of *every* characteristic we can observe in Real Socialism? Yes, according to Kornai: "The chief regularities of the system can be deduced" from the power structure dominated by the party; it "forms the deepest layer in the causal chain explaining the system."[30]

GROWTH AND BUREAUCRATIC COORDINATION

What comes next in that causal chain? Consider the goals of the vanguard within the social contract. Within the constraint of job rights, not only must sufficient consumption goods be produced to meet the current requirements for workers but productive capacity must expand enough to build the basis for the further development of socialism as well as satisfy the norm for future growth of consumption. The party thus must use its state power and state ownership of the means of production to expand productive forces. "The top leaders," Kornai argues, "want to impose with an iron hand a policy of the fastest possible growth," and "medium- and lower-level members of the bureaucracy are imbued by the same political conviction as the leaders."[31]

How is this to be done? Through "as large a scale of investment as possible." Though the level of present consumption is important, this is at most "a curb on the top leadership's inner impulse to maximize the proportion of investment."[32] Given its view that the development of productive forces is in the interest of satisfying future needs of the working class, the vanguard looks upon a surplus of use-values over and above current consumption requirements as purely *technical*, as a division between the present and future needs of workers. Accordingly, it extracts as much surplus as possible in the interest of the working class; the *raison d'être* of the vanguard, after all, is to lead the working class. Thus, Kornai argues, "The central leadership's decision in favor of a high investment proportion expresses the desire and purpose of the whole power elite."[33]

Naturally, the means by which its "inner impulse" are pursued are not selected randomly by the vanguard: "A specific political structure and ideology have gained sway, as a result of which specific property forms have developed, which has led to the preponderance of bureaucratic coordination and the typical behavior patterns of the participants."[34]

This "bureaucratic coordination," "a collection of specific social relations" characteristic of the sphere of production in Real Socialism, mirrors the pattern of party hierarchy.[35] Within the economy, Kornai noted, "relations of superiority-subordination between the individual or organization coordinating and the individual or organizations being coordinated" prevail; and the most typical flow of information is the "command, the order from the superior that the subordinate is required to obey."[36]

But what is to be coordinated? Everything. Recall the orchestra conductor: his success depends upon his ability to see the whole picture, to know what each player should be doing and to intervene to correct individual failures. In the same way, the bureaucracy is always prepared to intervene in the economy in order to achieve its goals. Faced with "spontaneous actions that the bureaucracy does not consider desirable," the natural response of the vanguard is to attempt to improve bureaucratic coordination, to increase regulations, etc. "The tendency to be complete, comprehensive, and watertight reappears constantly under the social conditions of bureaucratic coordination."[37]

Indeed, this is a spontaneous tendency of the bureaucracy, one that requires no central command; when things go wrong, every member of the bureaucracy understands what is to be done. If anything appears outside control, it must be controlled:

> If there is something amiss in these areas, each thinks: there must be fuller intervention to restore order. Each in his or her own field constantly reinforces the tendency described earlier as the completion of bureaucratic control, that is, preventing phenomena undesired by the bureaucracy from slipping through the net of rules, prescriptions, and bans.[38]

Thus the natural tendency of the vanguard is to "perfect" the methods of bureaucratic coordination. "The inevitable consequence," Kornai notes, "is proliferation of the bureaucracy. The expanded reproduction of the bureaucracy continues."[39] Indeed, he proposes, it was ever thus; citing Lenin's own complaints in 1921, Kornai calls attention to the "spontaneous self-generation, self-propagation, and excessive expansion of bureaucratic mechanisms that went beyond the expectations even of those who initiated and directed the epoch-making changes."[40]

THE SPECIFICALLY VANGUARD MODE OF PRODUCTION

Given, then, that "the system's internal logic propels bureaucratic power toward 'perfectionism'," the ultimate form of organization latent in the vanguard is the "direct, instruction-based bureaucratic control of a command-economy nature." At the heart of the directive central plan—"a monumental piece of bureaucratic coordination aimed at prior reconciliation of the processes of the economy"—is the attempt to coordinate and control the entire economy as "a single, nationwide 'factory'" directed from a single center. Of course, to implement the plan, "the chief method used by the higher authority to control the lower in all the decision-making and management spheres . . . is the command."[41]

Rather than central planning as such, once again this is central planning in its vanguard form. Its characteristic reliance upon centralized organization, control, and intervention flows directly from the vanguard relation—that relation in which the top/center asserts the correctness of direction from above and commands compliance. Here again, Kornai's logical construction yields a significant inference. He rejects the simplistic view that the problems of Real Socialism flowed from planning as such: "The features of the system cannot be derived from the fact that it is not a market economy, or still less from the fact that prices are irrational, and so on."[42]

On the contrary, command-planning of the economy as a single factory is derived from the genetic program of hierarchical control we have seen in the vanguard party:

> Direct bureaucratic control of the economy . . . embraces the elaboration
> of plans with the force of commands and the administrative compulsion
> to implement them, the management based on the commands, and the
> practice of the superior organization intervening regularly in every detail
> of the production and allocation processes and day-to-day running of
> the subordinate organization.[43]

The command-planning mechanism represents the development of a "specifically vanguard mode of production." However, at the outset its character is necessarily inadequate. As in the case of the development of manufacturing and the initial development of the factory within capitalism, this new mode of production is initially dependent upon characteristics it inherits. Just as capital needed to free itself from the skilled craftsman and to build machines with machines, so must the vanguard free itself from skilled intermediaries for this mode of production to grow by leaps and bounds.

For the vanguard to be able to direct the economy as a single nation-wide "factory," it must be certain that all the information it requires for planning is transmitted accurately from below and consolidated and that all its decisions on production (sectoral distribution and growth) are transmitted accurately downward to each unit of production. And all of this must be done in a timely manner without the individual players being able to deviate from the score. But this requires the *perfection* of the specifically vanguard mode of production—a computerized, cybernetic economy, "computopia"!

In short, the development of a single automated system of control is the condition for the perfection of direction from above of the national factory. In the fully developed vanguard mode of production, other than individual consumers whose atomistic decisions are reflected in inventory movements, only the vanguard has the power to use its discretion. Only the vanguard can make decisions with respect to the plan (and that includes a political decision not to follow the effect of consumer preferences—that is, politics are in command). In short, the ultimate decisions are made at the top. Once made, the mechanical orchestra will carry them out—the conductor will have the perfect orchestra.

The Organic System of Vanguard Relations

With the perfection of this vanguard mode of production, what could prevent the expanded reproduction of the system? Not only can computers produce other computers but, rather than the worker stepping to the side of the production process to watch the machine, computers can watch computers. Ever-growing productivity would be the result, and the vanguard would deliver not only the use-values necessary to satisfy its present and future obligations under the social contract but also the conditions necessary to approach the vanguard's promised society.

With the perfection of the vanguard mode of production, Real Socialism would be able to produce its own premises. Workers would be able to consume more and more and work less and less because implicit in this vanguard relation is the promise of limitless consumption and the concept of work as a burden. A world of abundance, "the realm of freedom"—all delivered by the vanguard. Workers would accept the rule of the vanguard party because it delivers what they want in this relationship.

In this organic system, every economic relation presupposes every other in its vanguard form, and everything posited is also a presupposition. Thus we see here a system whose elements are "organically connected and reinforce each other": a party of the vanguard-type, state ownership in its vanguard-form, state coordination in its vanguard-form, central planning of a vanguard-type, social and civic organizations of a vanguard-type, and, of course, an underlying population that *accepts* all this.

Though the vanguard party is the starting point for this logical construction, we understand that an organic system is not a linear sequence; rather, each part of the system acts upon every other—"the case with every organic whole."[44] Thus the vanguard party in this whole is not independent of the other parts. The party itself is acted upon; it is affected by the development of its undivided rule within the state, the nature of state ownership, and the responsibilities it takes on for coordination and central planning. With the completion of the organic system of vanguard relations of production, all of the hierarchical tendencies of the vanguard party are reinforced.[45]

The nature of that organic system, though, points to its inadequacies from a *socialist* perspective. Certainly, from its outset, this is a system of exploitation. Despite the vanguard's view that the existence and extent of extracted surplus is simply a technical division on behalf of the working class between meeting their present and future needs, the workers *themselves* have no power to make this choice. Rather, it is made for them by "those who know better." Thus this surplus product is the result of what Mészáros called the "political extraction of surplus labour."[46] And the ultimate destination of that surplus cannot change what it is. Even *if* workers were to be the sole recipients of this surplus product (that is, consume everything that was first extracted), the surplus would still be the result of the particular exploitation inherent in this vanguard relation.

To the extent that workers are the ultimate beneficiaries of the extractions, exploitation is reduced as a burden. Indeed, we may suggest that, within the organic system of vanguard relations (the system as "completed"), it would be secondary to the inherent *deformation* of people within such a society. The development of the vanguard mode of production "develops a working class which by education, tradition and habit looks upon the requirements of that mode of production as self-evident natural laws."[47]

What kinds of people are developed in the society of the conductor and the conducted? That is a society with a profound difference between thinking and doing, one where workers do not develop their potential because they do not engage in protagonistic activity. It is an alienated society in which workers do not view work as fulfilling, are alienated from the means of production, wish to consume and consume, and look upon work as a disutility—a burden that must be reduced. It is a society that cannot produce socialist human beings.

Is a system that produces such people sustainable—even with the full development of the specifically vanguard mode of production? This question, though, is abstract and speculative. More relevant here is the question of how vanguard relations of production are reproduced in the *absence* of computopia—that is, where the system is still dependent upon inherited premises.

Tendencies Within the Vanguard Mode of Regulation

In the chronological interim before the perfection of the specifically vanguard mode of production, those at the top rely upon a human chain of command rather than electronic signals. Through "bureaucratic coordination," those "relations of superiority-subordination" between individuals and institutions, functionaries in both enterprises and state coordinating agencies carry out decisions of those above them in the hierarchy. For successful execution of those decisions, the conductor must be inside the head of every player; and, the willingness of the members of this structure "to obey him makes it possible for the conductor to transform them into a unit, which he then embodies."

In practice, of course, the conductor *cannot* know what each player is doing at any moment and cannot respond to every situation his subordinates face. So the answer is rules for all subordinates. Rules, norms, and designated procedures must be established to cover all contingencies so the players know what to do. As long as they follow those rules, the members of this structure can be secure in the knowledge that they are doing the right thing. Any condition that falls outside those rules, however, produces a potential dilemma. The first response is denial—"No, it is not possible." If that does not dispose of the problem, the next resort is evasion—to pass the problem upward to the next person in the hierarchy. As Kornai described the behavior of those functioning within the structure, "It does not pay to think for oneself or take risks on one's own."

Despite a tendency toward paralysis for conditions outside the rules (and the predictable frustration this causes), the social contract ensures the continued acceptance of the power of the vanguard party so long as workers receive rising income, stability, and are assured of their job rights (that is, their near-absolute assurance of job security). In this respect, the social contract is a successful mode of regulation of vanguard relations. However, it compels the vanguard to expand both present and future consumption and investment in order to satisfy the social contract and to develop the productive forces that are the condition for building the new society.

What are the possibilities for success? If these relations with their inherent tendency for expanded reproduction exist alongside forms of production characterized by earlier productive relations (for example, small peasant agriculture), then there is enormous potential for expansion by detaching labor and material resources from those earlier forms and incorporating them within production under vanguard relations. The expanded reproduction of vanguard relations here has as its counterpart the contracted reproduction of those other relations. Although he ignores the latter side, Kornai is correct in his comment that "in mobilizing labour as the most important resource of society, in systematically bringing labour into the production process the socialist economy proves to be highly efficient." This, he admitted, is "one of its most important historical achievements."[48]

Recall, though, Kornai's original argument about the shortage economy—that the reproduction of shortages "is ultimately related to impatient chasing of economic growth, the forcing of the acceleration of the growth rate."[49] With the system's high production targets and high demand for labor and resources, he argued that there was an inherent tendency to generate shortages. However, the source of this tendency within the social contract is not only the result of the demand side. When trying to develop the productive forces rapidly, the vanguard comes up against supply constraints inherent in the nature of that contract.

For one, "the virtually complete job security" of workers—the package of job rights that gave them security of their particular employment and a relatively leisurely pace of work—necessarily affects the supply side.[50] Further, to the extent that workers could neither be dismissed nor compelled "to work at trades other than those for which they were employed when hired," it affected the pattern of investment. Planners, according to Granick, were "reluctant to engage in substantial labour saving investments in existing plants, because it is never clear ahead of time whether such investments could actually be put into use."[51]

But those planners can make the decision to build new factories and infrastructure and can feel secure that their subordinates will mobilize resources to carry out those decisions. Precisely because workers actively defend their job rights, expansion of production tends to occur by combining new means of production with workers in new workplaces rather than through introduction of labor-saving technology in existing workplaces.[52] Characteristic of the law of motion within this social contract, in short, is the *tendency for extensive rather than intensive growth*.

Naturally, expanded reproduction benefits greatly from the ability to siphon resources and labor from preexisting productive relations. However, though an extensive growth path clearly benefits from such labor reserves, it is not entirely dependent upon them: the new, superior workplaces can attract workers by providing better working conditions, wages, and benefits. After all, this social contract includes the right of individual workers to follow their material interest and to change jobs. Job rights only ensure that they are not *compelled* to change either their jobs or their place of employment. In sum, there is a labor market—but it is a "*sellers'* market" which, as Lewin commented, allows workers to "defend their interests by changing jobs."[53]

Consider the "law of motion" characteristic of this process. Given its production of atomistic, alienated consumer-workers who want to minimize work and maximize consumption, the system requires continuing quantitative expansion. Following an extensive growth model, however, implies that *sooner or later* the system will approach limits in resources and labor supplies. The point at which this would tend to occur, of course, differs—depending, for example, on the extent to which previous development in a particular country had absorbed those labor and resource reserves.

Under the above conditions, all other things equal, a lower rate of growth is likely. As Kornai concluded from his macroeconomic model of the shortage economy, "The exhaustion of labour reserves is sufficient in itself to force the economic system to leave its old growth path for a newer and much slower one."[54] All the norms associated with the social contract are now threatened: *"All norms have to adjust to accommodate the new situation,* but this will not take place without resistance."[55] After all, as cited in chapter 2, "holding back increases in living standards or their absolute reduction . . . sooner or later entails serious political and social consequences."[56] At what point does dissatisfaction begin? "And, if there is dissatisfaction, at what point it starts to endanger the stability of the system. It is a historical fact that unrest may be so great that it induces leaders to change economic policy."[57]

Unexplained Variations

We should not be too quick to conclude that the social contract was the source of all the phenomena associated with the shortage economy of Real Socialism or that it alone generated growing shortages and the threats to the continuation of this social contract.

After all, what in this description of the social contract (and, indeed, of vanguard relations of production) would explain the production of heavy chandeliers and "gold-plated" coats? What does a tendency of "management of enterprises to loosen plans, to hide production potentials, and to hold back outstanding production achievements" have to do with vanguard relations as such? As Kornai indicated in the 1950s, "This is highly dangerous and harmful." So why would the vanguard want this and allow it to continue? Given the dependence of the vanguard mode of production upon accurate information, how is the tendency to send false information not dysfunctional?

As soon as we pose such questions, we are necessarily brought back with a jolt to recall the existence and behavior of the enterprise managers who are *outside* this particular social contract between the vanguard and the working class. In the absence of the fully developed vanguard mode of production, the complete information required for central planning of the economy as a single factory is not available. So, what mechanism was chosen in Real Socialism to encourage enterprise managers to carry out the goals of the vanguard? Material incentives—bonuses. We have already seen an unintended consequence of this mechanism—the fostering of a *different* relation and of a different logic that interacts with the logic of vanguard relations.

4—Contested Reproduction in Real Socialism

As we have seen, Kornai argued that Real Socialism was an organic system—a system whose "combination of main features forms an organic whole," a "coherent system," "a coherent whole" whose elements are "organically connected and reinforce each other."[1] Precisely because its elements "all belong together and strengthen each other," he insisted that the system could not be partially reformed but had to be replaced.[2]

But Kornai was not the only one who argued that Real Socialism was an organic system. That was official ideology, as demonstrated by Richard Kosolapov, a Soviet supporter of Real Socialism. Drawing specifically upon Marx's discussion of organic systems, he argued that socialism becomes a totality by subordinating all elements of society to itself and by creating the new organs it needs—that is, by producing its own premises and preconditions. It becomes an organic social system, Kosolapov explained, through its development of the productive forces that ensure a socialized economy "in fact" and thus a "natural mutual correspondence" between the elements of the system. And that stage indeed had now occurred: "The stage when the system becomes a totality is the stage of developed socialism." Thus we see here the argument for Real Socialism as a completed and stable social system—resulting, in Brezhnev's words, in "the organic integrity and dynamic force of the social system, its political stability, its indestructible inner unity."[3]

Both the critic and the advocate of Real Socialism, though, were wrong. Our description of the struggle between vanguard and managers reveals that it was *not* a single, coherent system, "a structure in which all the elements coexist simultaneously and support one another." Rather than an "inner coherence," there was contested reproduction in Real Socialism—the result of the logic of different systems it contained and which interacted to generate dysfunction.

Certainly, there's nothing unique about pointing out the "distinction between the enterprise and the center" and emphasizing how "decisions of enterprise managers will lead to results which are dysfunctional from the viewpoint of the central authorities."[4] Indeed, the picture of the enterprise managers presented in chapter 1 was so familiar to analysts of Real Socialism that Granick could describe it in his 1975 book as "the orthodox model."[5] In that model, the managers are treated as "independent and maximizing decision makers" who "suboptimize with regard to society's goals as these are perceived by central authorities." Further, that model stressed the "suboptimizing behavior by individual enterprises which lead to macroeconomic malfunctioning."[6]

Although that "orthodox model" acknowledged a parallel between the income-maximizing behavior of managers in Real Socialism and the profit-maximization assumption for firms within capitalism, it did not proceed from there to call the managers capitalists. And, on its face, it *should* not. After all, these managers didn't own the means of production, didn't have the power to compel workers to perform surplus labor, and didn't own commodities (as a result of the labor process) that could be exchanged to realize surplus value which can be the basis for the accumulation of capital. Further, under the social contract they lacked the ability to drive down real wages, intensify the labor process, and introduce labor-saving technology. In short, we do not find here capitalist relations of production.

However, these managers do contain within them the *logic of capital*—just as merchant and moneylending capitalists did before capital was successful in seizing possession of production. Whereas the existing constraints upon the managers do not permit us to classify them as capitalists, the drive, impulse, the *logic* of these managers is a different matter. If these income-maximizing managers struggle to remove the constraints placed upon them—for example, specific output targets, designated suppliers and customers, the appropriation of enterprise profits, the inability to discipline or fire workers, or to introduce freely new methods of production, what is this drive if *not* the logic of capital? Expressing that logic is the mantra—*Free capital!*

The Interaction of the Two Logics

What happens when two differing logics coexist? In the 1920s, Evgeny Preobrazhensky argued that the state economy in the USSR was in "an uninterrupted economic war with the tendencies of capitalist development, with the tendencies of capitalist restoration."[7] This, he proposed, was a "struggle between two mutually hostile systems," a war between two regulating principles—one the result of the spontaneous effects of commodity-capitalist relations ("the law of value") and the other based upon the conscious decisions of the regulatory organs of the state (which he called "the law of primitive socialist accumulation").[8]

Preobrazhensky argued that each of these regulating principles was "fighting for the type of regulation which is organically characteristic of the particular system of production-relations, taken in its pure form." However, the result of their interaction, he proposed, was that the Soviet economy in the 1920s was regulated by *neither* in its pure form. There was no simple combination or addition of the productive relations and their associated regulating principles; rather, Preobrazhensky insisted, they *interpenetrated*—coexisting, limiting, and (significantly) deforming each other.[9]

In short, two systems and two logics do not simply exist side-by-side. They *interact*. They interpenetrate. And they deform each other. Rather than the combination permitting the best of both worlds, the effect can be the worst of the two worlds. Precisely because there is contested reproduction between differing sets of productive relations, the interaction of the systems can generate crises, inefficiencies, and irrationality that wouldn't be found in either system in its purity.

This is the unarticulated story of Real Socialism—that its particular characteristics were the result of neither the logic of the vanguard nor the logic of capital. Rather, it was the particular combination of the two which yielded the dysfunction and deformation identified with Real Socialism.

THE LAW OF VALUE
AND THE LAW OF COMMAND

To understand the interaction of the two logics, we need to consider not only each logic but also how it is executed by individual actors. Recall the logic of capital in capitalism once it is fully developed. Given capital's drive for self-expansion, its inherent tendency is to increase the rate of exploitation by driving up the workday in length and intensity, driving down the real wage, increasing productivity (specifically, relative to the real wage), and by separating and dividing workers in order to weaken them. Further, capital constantly attempts to expand its ability to realize surplus value contained in commodities by expanding its sphere of circulation and creating new needs. The self-expansion of capital also means the attempt to reduce its requirements in both the sphere of production (thus substitution of machinery for labor) and the sphere of circulation (thus efforts to reduce the time of circulation) as well as choosing those sectors for accumulation that maximize the growth of capital.

By grasping the nature of capital, we see its inherent tendency for an increase in the technical composition of capital (and intensive development), expansion of needs and the market (for example, the world market), for accumulation of capital (and, indeed, for overaccumulation because the expansion of capital occurs without regard for the conditions for realization). However, this understanding comes from the logical development of the concept of capital. In the real world, there is no single actor, capital in general, that pursues these goals directly. Rather, it appears that individual capitals are driven by competition and generate these results. The inner laws of capital necessarily appear to individual capitalists as external coercive laws. [10]

To compete with other capitalists who are equally driven by the desire for profits, the individual capitalist must lower his costs. He must reduce his labor costs; thus he tries to get a greater quantity of labor for a given expenditure on wages by increasing the workday and driving down wages (perhaps by moving to where labor will be cheaper). Further, relative to his competitors, he tries to reduce his costs of production in general (by substituting machinery for labor) and his costs of circulation (by innovating to reduce inventory requirements and speeding up sales). To make profits, of course, these individual capitalists must produce the things that will generate profits. Thus they will expand production in those areas for which demand is rising because, all other things equal, this will tend to generate rising prices and profits. Individual capitalists, accordingly, in their search for profits are driven by demand and by competition with other sellers—that is, *by the market*.

That demand, of course, is not the demand of abstract individual consumers. It reflects the nature of capitalist relations of production, and its pattern is affected by class struggle (for example, the distribution of income). Further, the market that drives individual capitalists is simply the logic of capital as it must appear to individual capitalists (that is, the necessary form of appearance of the inner law of capital). The essential character of capital, its drive for self-expansion (which includes the drive to economize upon capital and allocate the labor of society in such a way as to maximize self-expansion) takes the necessary form of market compulsion—in short, as the compulsion of "the law of value."

Consider, on the other hand, the logic of the vanguard. As we have seen, in its orientation toward building socialism, the vanguard seeks the most rapid possible development of productive forces. Kornai, accordingly, refers to "the top leadership's inner impulse to maximize the proportion of investment."[11] Following logically from this "inner impulse," the vanguard would want to minimize waste, inefficiency, and duplication of effort as well as slack and underemployment of people and resources. Further, to achieve that growth and meet the expectations of the underlying population, the vanguard needs to allocate labor between and within

Departments I (means of production) and II (articles of consumption). Finally, to make these decisions real, the logic of the vanguard calls for an economic plan that requires instruction and command from above.

Though there is a real actor that embodies the logic of the vanguard (that is, the vanguard party), there is also, as in the case of the logic of capital, a difference between inner laws and the interaction of real individual actors who execute those immanent laws. Consider the perspective of those individuals at the top of the state-party structure—in ministries, planning bodies, and other institutions contributing to the creation of the plan. In the pure form of the vanguard relation, each internalizes the perspective of the vanguard in general. Each seeks to build socialism through the development of productive forces and sees the necessity for discipline, centralization, and unity in order to achieve this. For those individual actors, the inner logic of the vanguard appears as a compulsion—*as responsibility and duty*, as the sense that everything depends upon them; and the result is that they "work long, hard hours in the firm belief that in doing so they serve the cause of their party and of the people, the common good and the interests of mankind."[12]

To best contribute to the goal of building socialism, each of those at the top wants to regulate closely all subordinates and wants more resources. Thus the creation and execution of the plan in practice reflects the interaction of those individual perspectives—through their demands for both greater resources and greater power over their subordinates. As the result of this combination, those who lead express the "inner impulse" of the vanguard to maximize investment and expand hierarchical control— "each thinks: there must be fuller intervention." Add managers of individual units of production who similarly internalize the perspective of the vanguard, and we can see the unfolding of the logic of the vanguard in its "pure" form.

There is, of course, a major difference between the way the logic of capital and the logic of the vanguard are executed. In contrast to the unconscious, spontaneous result that flows from the atomistic behavior of individual capitals, in the case of the vanguard there is a conscious collective commitment. Democratic centralism is the underlying mechanism, and though competing interests may enter into the formulation of the plan, once that plan is adopted, it is meant to be carried out and "instructions passed down from above must be carried out by the subordinates."[13] The logic of the vanguard takes the form of the administrative-directive plan, the "law" of command.

DYSFUNCTION IN REAL SOCIALISM

What happens when the logic of the vanguard and the logic of capital interact? When commands are issued by those at the top, they are received by managers who embody not the logic of the vanguard but the logic of capital. Those managers do not proceed from their recognition of the interdependence between their production targets and the predetermined plan as a whole. On the contrary, income-maximizing managers act in their own individual interests. However, they are not free to pursue their own interests under conditions of their own choosing. Those managers are constrained by vanguard relations, and the logic of capital requires them to remove those constraints. In the struggle between these two logics, we can see the basis for the phenomena of the shortage economy.

Consider, for example, how the logic of capital is affected as the result of the law of command. In attempting to maximize the income they can obtain through their access to the means of production, the managers are constrained by instructions from the vanguard, by the law of command. But this is a *myopic* command, and accordingly, their entrepreneurial activity involves taking advantage of that myopia.

The combination of self-interested managerial behavior and myopia at the top allows, as we have seen, the managers to take advantage of plan ambiguities to earn bonuses while directing the production of perverse outputs (for example, those heavy chandeliers and "gold-plated" coats). And the same combination infects the plan itself. Since managerial income is not based simply upon compliance with an externally imposed enterprise plan, negotiation of the production target is an object of entrepreneurial activity. Thus the managers lie and distort information sent upward. As part of this same pattern, the "wise director" underproduces relative to his potential. Here is where, as Šik indicated, "people's initiative could really develop to the full." How can you plan accurately on the basis of such information?

This is not, however, a matter of the inherent inefficiency of central planning or of the technical incapacity to obtain and utilize the information essential for planning. *Bad information in this case reflects class struggle.* Kornai aptly described the result in the 1950s: "In a word, present planning and incentive systems have evoked a spontaneous tendency, the effect of which is to induce managements of enterprises to loosen plans, to hide production potentials, and to hold back outstanding production achievements. This is highly dangerous and harmful."[14] But why was this occurring? Very simply, those dangerous and harmful outcomes to which Kornai referred were explicitly the product of a particular combination of *two different logics*—in a word, the "present planning" system (the logic of the vanguard) and the "incentive" system (the logic of capital).

These systemic dysfunctions were not the only harmful outcomes. Certainly the waste from "storming" and the shortages produced by the stockpiling of resources and workers were inherent in the logic of capital when subject to the law of myopic command. But it also was entirely rational for managers to do whatever was necessary to have more workers and resources on hand to meet targets (for example, "every manager tries to wring higher wages for his shop, section, etc., from his superior."). Rather than driven to lower their labor and material costs by the law of value, the managers create conditions by which they instead can maximize both resource and labor supplies within their own units, even though this is not rational for the society as a whole.

All this flows from what Kornai called "the joint effects of plan instructions and incentives." By itself, the orientation of the planners was characteristic of "a coherent, unified mechanism, which has its own inner logic and several tendencies and regularities peculiar to itself."[15] We see, though, that that logic did not exist by itself. There was also the logic characteristic of the managers; and in the conflict between the managers' sense of responsibility to the total economy and their own economic interest, Kornai proposed that "it is only human, if individual economic interest proves to be stronger."[16] Precisely because the logic of capital is "only human," Kornai concluded that it was *only rational* to free that logic from the constraints of the vanguard.

Consider the other side—how the logic of the vanguard is affected by the behavior of the managers. Those at the top of the state-party structure know that they cannot depend upon obedience, upon loyalty to the vanguard, and upon a sense of responsibility on the part of existing managers to the social interest. Indeed, they know that the interests of those managers differ and that the managers have knowledge the vanguard does not have (the differing interests and the myopia that are, of course, the premise for the principal-agent problem discussed in chapter 2). To achieve the goal, then, of maximizing production by mobilizing resources and labor to that end, the vanguard must factor in the behavior of individual managers.

Accordingly, the vanguard at every level must stress "taut" plans (which increase on the basis of "achieved results") and reduced input norms—precisely because of the high probability of the hidden reserves and the "bogus difficulties" claimed by the managers. But by how much? *As much as possible.* Given their lack of accurate information and the real shortages reflecting managerial behavior, there is a tendency for assigned plans to go beyond what is feasible. Further, because of the perverse production patterns generated by bonus-maximizing managerial activity, more regulations and norms (covering, for example, product variety, product quality, productivity, wage bills, etc.) are logical.[17] Thus more information that an overburdened center needs to digest.

All these responses from above (accompanied by the multiplication of a bureaucracy to attempt to monitor and enforce targets and regulations), of course, only intensify a tendency to generate plan failures and shortages. And that fosters *further* initiative on the part of the managers. Faced with the prospect of not getting planned delivery of necessary inputs and thus not securing their bonuses, the logical answer for these managers is to go *outside* the plan. Accordingly, it becomes individually rational for enterprises to produce their own essential inputs and to engage in barter transactions with other enterprises to trade excess inventory of some inputs in exchange for their own requirements. Not only is this a resort to an undeveloped form of commodity exchange (which gives rise to specialists in supplies, the *tolkachi*) but production for the purpose of exchange (and thus an additional diversion of resources) can soon follow. As Kagarlitsky commented with respect to the Soviet Union: "Informal barter, far from solving the fundamental problems of production, complicated them by encouraging the formation of additional reserves. This in turn led to an exacerbation of shortages."[18]

How can one talk about a central plan in this context? The concept of the central plan is an attempt to coordinate all aspects of the economy by considering in advance the interdependencies of all subunits and linking consumer goods production and income in order to ensure macroeconomic balances. However, when the managers go outside the plan to stockpile resources and labor (thereby contributing to shortages), produce their own input requirements (contributing to economic irrationality), and waste physical, human, and monetary resources by directing their enterprises to engage in "storming" (thereby producing low quality or useless products), we can see the dysfunctional character of Real Socialism. In Flaherty's words, it is a "structure in which a central command is given and spontaneous administrative processes then take over."[19]

Describing the disintegration of coherent planning in Poland, Maziarski pointed to the inability of those at the top to "conduct any sort of coordinated policy because departments with greater access to the policy-making process lobbied for their investments, destroyed the logic of the plan, and ruined any chance of escape from the crisis."[20] The attempt to coordinate the entire economy as a single, nationwide factory fails when there is self-oriented behavior by those who possess the individual means of production; it fails just as an attempt to coordinate from above within a single vertically integrated factory would fail if there were commodity exchange by independent, autonomous producers at every stage of production in that factory.

Plan failures, though, are not random. All industries are not equal; some do have a higher priority than others even in a well-coordinated plan. Accordingly, some are more likely to face a soft budget constraint than others. In a situation of sporadic and growing shortages, the vanguard needs to be certain that scarce inputs are allocated to the most critical sectors, those whose linkages to the rest of the economy are greatest (and thus whose plan failures would have the greatest impact). The high-priority sectors, accordingly, will tend not to be those producing consumer goods; therefore, plan failures (and revised plans) tend to cluster in these sectors—even though the social contract may require increased output of consumer goods.[21]

In short, chronic shortage for consumers—"every member of the household is recommended to carry a shopping bag." We are back at our concrete starting point—and this time we understand it as a rich totality of many relations. This time, we understand it as the result of a "struggle between two mutually hostile systems," where each of the two logics is "fighting for the type of regulation which is organically characteristic of the particular system of production-relations, taken in its pure form."[22]

DEFORMATION IN REAL SOCIALISM

The problem, though, is not simply that this struggle between two opposite logics generates dysfunction. There is also the question of the effect of this interaction upon each side. In the combination and interaction between two logics, neither the managers nor the vanguard exist in a vacuum; in that interaction, each is deformed .

Bihari, considering the perspective of factory managers in Hungarian market reform debates, described the deformation of the logic of capital well: "In principle, the factory managers sympathize with the radical market solution, since *in the long term it would result in the enhancement of their economic and political power*. They would be the principal winners in 'marketization.'" However, "in practice there are few of them who actually prefer economic independence" because of the fear that they would not be able to compete on the market. "These fears make a number of factory managers supporters of the status quo."[23] For individual managers, in short, this distinction between "in principle" (the logic of capital) and "in practice" with respect to the full development of market reforms reflects the deforming effect of interaction of the logic of capital with the logic of the vanguard. The law of value here gives way to a law of *lobbying*—a competition for access to resources.

A similar development can be seen on the side of the vanguard. What are those individuals at the top of the state-party structure (in ministries, planning bodies, etc.) to do when faced with the prospect of shortages producing plan failures? Their commitment to the project as a whole leads them first of all to attempt to insulate their own institutions from failures—that is, to control what is in their immediate power to control. One manifestation of this tendency is the pattern of "departmentalism" described by Kagarlitsky:

> Bureaucratic institutions operate according to the principle of "everyone for themselves." In distributing their products, all are governed by the principle of "your own first." This leads to the famous "counter-transportation" where a factory sends its production not to its immediate neighbour but to the other end of the country—because that is where there is an enterprise from the same department, while the neighbour belongs to another one. Different ministries create production of the same type within their own system just so they do not have to depend on each other.[24]

With growing shortages, the response of ministries and production associations becomes one of "anticipatory competition," a struggle to ensure that their sub-units secure the resources they needed. Thus a gulf emerges here between the needs of the system as seen by those at the center and the needs for self-sufficiency as perceived by those lower down in the production chain: "The central authorities are primarily concerned with maximizing long-term growth while subordinate agencies concentrate their energies on short-term objectives and advantages."[25]

If the autonomous activity of enterprise managers chronically infects the plan, how can those who have the responsibility of overseeing the portion of the plan entrusted to them minimize the effect of the infection? Not only departmentalism but also finding ways to enable enterprises under their authority to produce as much as possible follows. Thus, in contrast to demanding the highest possible targets in the conception and creation of the annual plans, those at the top of the vanguard at this point see the necessity to induce the managers to meet plan targets. To prevent managers from "losing all hope" at securing their bonuses, plan targets are adjusted downward within the plan period itself in order to be more realistic. Further, those at the top look the other way when it comes to the various questionable and illegal measures pursued by managers to facilitate plan-fulfillment—that is, they *acquiesce* in the waste, stockpiling of labor and resources, and duplication of effort that is contrary to the inner impulse of the vanguard. With growing shortages and plan failures, the law of command is increasingly transformed into a law of *enablement*—another aspect of the deformation of the logic of the vanguard.

Thus, in contrast to the hierarchy inherent in vanguard relations, when it comes to realization of the plan the relationship between vanguard and managers is inverted. Those at the top are dependent (and recognize that dependence) upon the enterprises to deliver their portion of the central plan. On the other hand, the enterprise managers chafe under the constraints of the vanguard but also develop a growing sense of their independence and power to the extent that they are able to achieve their goals despite the controls over them. This (Hegelian) inversion is precisely why we could consider the managers as the "principals" in their relation with the planners, and it is the context in which the sectoral coalitions and the pattern of sectoral dominance flourished, as described in chapter 3.[26]

Thus we see here a definite tendency for the line between the two opposites to become blurred in practice—that is, a tendency for an identity of opposites to emerge. On the one hand, there are managers hesitant to pursue the logic of capital fully; on the other, we see planners who support the actions of self-oriented managers. Though the coming together of these opposites can provide mutual security for a time and can generate an apparent stabilization within Real Socialism, that unity is only apparent. What prevails is the now hidden, now open *struggle* between the two logics—a struggle in particular over property, that is, the ownership of the means of production.

PROPERTY, PLAN, AND MARKET

The struggle takes the form of a struggle between plan and market. It is a struggle not over juridical ownership but over *real* ownership of the means of production: what does it mean to own?

Though a popular conception tends to think of ownership as undivided, it is generally accepted by those who study property that ownership involves a bundle of different property rights that are often not held by a single party.[27] Drawing upon property rights literature, for example, Kornai identified as key elements: (1) the right to the residual income (and to decide how to use it); (2) the right of alienation or transferability (to rent, sell, bequeath, etc.); and (3) the right to control (including the right to delegate that control). Considering Real Socialism, he noted that "the power elite, hierarchically structured and sharing power with no other group, has the exclusive right of disposal over the state-owned means of production."[28]

But one part of that bundle did not appear to be present. According to Andras Hegedus (former prime minister of Hungary), the state bureaucracy exercised the power to direct people, to dispose of the means of production, and the almost unlimited power to use and distribute the surplus product through its hierarchically arranged decision-making system—that is, it had all those attributes of ownership. However, it *lacked* the power to sell, bequeath, or alienate the means of production. This led Hegedus to describe the state bureaucracy in Real Socialism as the *possessor* rather than the proprietor.[29]

As a general principle, Hegedus stressed that "we must always ask whether there exists some kind of real control over those who dispose of power and exercise possession in the name of the proprietor."[30] Since in Real Socialism society as a whole was the juridical owner (that is, the proprietor), then the question in this case was whether there was control over the state bureaucracy. Indeed, Hegedus argued, "the core of the problem of property" was the struggle for "the replacement of possession by the state administration with ownership-exercise by society as a whole." Accordingly, Hegedus stressed the necessity of a struggle for democracy—that is, for real control over the possessor by strengthening democratic forms of administration.[31]

Yet Hegedus was well aware that there was a different and immediate challenge to the existing possession of the means of production. There was a "rapidly advancing form"—a *different* distribution of property rights that was emerging: "possession by the managerial administration of the enterprise." The managers of enterprises, he noted, exercise their "possession in the field of property with a relatively high degree of independence."[32] And, this possession by the managers, he proposed, advances at the expense of possession by the state administration. That encroachment was, "of course, a process that is accompanied by sharp conflicts. Those organs of state administration which have exercised possession up to that point do everything in their power to maintain their old policies."[33]

Like Hegedus, Charles Bettelheim also identified the struggle between the managers and state administration as a struggle over property rights. Though he also stressed the essential distinction between "possession" and ownership, Bettelheim defined possession differently—as "the *ability to put the means of production into operation*."[34] Thus possession for him involved the technical capacity in a specific site to carry out and direct a labor process. "Every unit of production," Bettelheim argued, "forms a *center* for the appropriation of nature. Within such a center, different labor processes are closely articulated; thus every unit of production actually has the capacity to utilize its means of production, which it consequently *possesses*."[35]

Property and ownership, accordingly, must be distinguished from possession in Bettelheim's sense. Property involves "*the power to appropriate* the objects on which it acts for uses that are given, particularly the *means of production*, and the power to dispose of the products obtained with the help of those means of production." And, for that power of property (those property rights) to be effective, the agents of property must rule: either they must possess the means of production themselves or the agents of possession must be "subordinated to the agents of property."[36] The critical struggle over property for Bettelheim, accordingly, was between the owners (the agents of property) and *would-be* owners (those who possess units of production).

So who owns the means of production within Real Socialism? *It depends.* It depends upon the relative strength of the contending parties. The state, Bettelheim argued, is able to act as proprietor of the means of production when "these means are directly brought under control and put into operation," and this occurs through the "*plan* and the planned relations that are derived from this plan."[37] The more the state coordinates *a priori* the different units of production, the more those who possess the means of production are subordinated to the state as proprietor.[38]

In short, the plan is the way that enterprises are prevented from transforming their possession into property. The state acts as owner "on the one hand when state property effectively enables the governmental authorities to 'reappropriate' all or part of what each enterprise possesses; on the other hand, when the state effectively *dominates* the use that the enterprises make of their means of production and products." The state thus dominates through the central plan: "The *state's power to dispose of products and appropriate the means of production*" is "the effect of specific *relations of production*, of *property relations*."[39]

Conversely, replacing the plan with the market is, as Hegedus formulated it, "the replacement of possession by state management with possession by enterprise management." As market prices are introduced "in place of the previous bureaucratic price," as management is enabled "to make the decisions concerning all the important questions of enterprise development (changes in the product structure, technical development, investment, etc.)," possession by the managers is strengthened.[40] From Bettelheim's perspective, indeed, such ability of enterprises to make their own decisions about the use of the means of production that they possess is "an effect of specific relations of production, that is, capitalist relations of production."[41]

This conflict between plan and market should not be identified as a struggle between socialist and capitalist relations of production. Domination via the central plan, Bettelheim noted, "can be *socialist relations* to the extent that they really ensure the *domination of workers* over the conditions of production and reproduction, and, therefore, over the means and results of their labor."[42] The state's powers over the means of production (that is, its property rights), he argued, "only constitutes an effect of socialist relations of production *insofar* as these powers really ensure the domination of the workers over the conditions of production and reproduction."[43] *As we have seen in our discussion, however, domination by workers over the conditions of production and reproduction is precisely what is precluded by vanguard relations of production.*

To the extent that the enterprise managers are prevented from turning their possession of the means of production into property, the vanguard is the collective owner of the means of production in Real Socialism. Its powers are the powers of owners: it determines the goal of production and directs people and means of production in order to achieve that goal, decides how and by whom the products of this activity will be enjoyed, and allocates the surplus over and above what is necessary to reproduce the conditions of production.[44]

Demonstrating its ownership, further, the vanguard is able to assign particular property rights to others. That is precisely what occurred within the social contract through the granting of job rights to workers. The protection from being fired or being forced to change their jobs against their will meant in practice that workers were linked to specific means of production. *In short, workers under the social contract possess particular property rights*—they have the right to continue to use those means of production or to shift jobs and establish a similar link to other means of production.[45]

Consider vanguard relations of production. In the absence of the specifically vanguard mode of production, their reproduction requires a mode of regulation that can ensure production of the premises of the system. Control of managers through the administrative-directive plan and the existence of the social contract constitute a specifically vanguard mode of regulation that allowed both the reproduction of the vanguard as the owner of the means of production and the reproduction of workers in their existing relation to the means of production. But a successful mode of regulation is not automatic—it is the terrain where contested reproduction occurs.

In the "struggle between two mutually hostile systems" that characterized Real Socialism, managers wanted to be "free." Free from all control, free from the "petty tutelage" of the vanguard, free from the constraints of the social contract (in particular, free from the ultimate constraint of job rights). Embodying the logic of capital, the managers emerged as a class oriented toward the transfer of all property rights over the means of production from both vanguard and the working class. Not surprisingly, their particular class interest was presented as the general interest—that is, as an end to irrationality.

5—The Conductor and the Battle of Ideas in the Soviet Union

Recall Canetti's description of the orchestra conductor:

> His eyes hold the whole orchestra. Every player feels that the conductor sees him personally, and still more, hears him. The voices of the instruments are opinions and convictions on which he keeps a close watch. He is omniscient, for, while the players have only their own parts in front of them, he has the whole score in his head, or on his desk. At any given moment he knows precisely what each player should be doing. His attention is everywhere at once, and it is to this that he owes a large part of his authority. He is inside the mind of every player. He knows not only what each *should* be doing, but also what he *is* doing. He is the living embodiment of law, both positive and negative. His hands decree and prohibit. His ears search out profanation.[1]

What happens, though, when the conductor is forced to admit that something has gone terribly wrong? When the conductor concludes that there is a problem with the music—"the only thing that counts"—what is to be done?

THE CONTEXT

Because of its importance for the understanding of the fate of Real Socialism, we will consider here the specific case of the Soviet Union. When two hostile systems interact, the result may be crises, inefficiencies, and an irrationality that wouldn't be found in either system in its purity. Rather than a "coherent whole" composed of elements that "mutually complement and attract each other," the interaction of the logic of the vanguard and the logic of capital produces something quite different. Indeed, what may emerge is the worst of both worlds.

Was this the situation in the Soviet Union? There can be little doubt about how dysfunctional its economy was—the waste, the stockpiling of labor and resources, the poor quality products, the extreme alienation and low productivity of workers, the lack of correct information to engage in planning, the departmentalism, the plan evasions, and the inability to control enterprise managers. And there is no absence of evidence pointing to a growing crisis—significantly falling growth rates from the 1950s through the 1980s, a declining efficiency of investment (that is, falling output-capital ratios), growing shortages of resources and labor, and falling productivity growth.[2]

It is tempting to explain the crisis simply by reference to labor shortages and to attribute these to the continuation of the extensive growth model. Certainly, there were obvious signs of labor shortages. In addition to evidence of growing job vacancies, there was an inability to utilize additions to industrial capacity in the 1960s and 1970s because of the lack of sufficient labor: "In the 1970s, a Gosplan research director reported that 10–12% of the increment in real fixed capital was unutilized due to a shortage of labour." Allen sums up the situation by commenting that "the capital stock rose without a corresponding rise in GDP because there was no labour to operate the new capacity."[3]

In general, sources of additional labor for Soviet industry were increasingly exhausted. By 1965, for example, it was already apparent to Gosplan investigators that the demand for labor was far outrunning the growth in labor supplies—"in other words, the requisite workers had been obtained mainly by drawing upon those working at home or on their private plots. . . .

But the number of those working at home was continuing to fall and this source would soon dry up."[4] Considering only demographic patterns, how long could the Soviet Union follow an extensive development model that depended upon continuing increments of labor to be combined with resources in new productive units without generating a crisis?

Yet the explanation of the crisis is not quite that simple. First of all, labor shortages have to be considered in the context of the managerial tendency to stockpile labor. Myasnikov, for example, argued in 1979 that "at most Soviet machinery plants, the number of employees is 30% to 50% higher than similar enterprises abroad."[5] Similarly, while Grancelli estimated in 1988 that "as a result of the hoarding of labour, the hidden labour reserves in industrial enterprises ranged from 10 to 20 per cent of total personnel," other sources suggested much larger stockpiling of workers in the USSR. Thus, Kuznetsov gave an example from the ammonium industry: "Several producers of ammonia, using the same technology and plant, were surveyed in Russia in 1983. According to a normative, the production needed manpower of 83. The actual employment ranged from the normative figure to as many as 230, 294 and even 490 in some enterprises."[6] As Filzer noted, there was a "seeming paradox of a severe and reproducible labour shortage alongside overstaffing within each individual production unit."[7]

Further, labor shortages were by no means universal. While they were marked in western and developed parts of the Soviet Union (especially in the Baltics) and Siberia, this was not the case in the Central Asian republics where population growth rates were twice the Soviet average. Yet despite the geographical disparities in labor shortages and surpluses, it appears that "labour availability was not taken into consideration" when planning the location of industrial plants. "Major labour-intensive industries had been located in regions where labour was scarce," and "regions with surplus labour had experienced reduced investment." The 1965 Gosplan report concluded that the deteriorating situation was "due in part to miscalculations by planning and economic agencies, and in part to errors in economic policy."[8] Very simply, the report indicated that "the employment factor is still not genuinely integrated into the formation of the national economic plan."[9]

It appears that such warnings were not sufficient to reverse the situation. Reflecting in part the employment of women in industry, inadequate housing, and insufficient childcare facilities, population growth in areas of labor scarcity continued to be low.[10] Meanwhile, the combination of continuing rapid population increase and relatively low economic expansion in non-European parts of the Soviet Union meant that by the mid-1980s, there was substantial long-term unemployment. In this situation, given the reluctance of Muslims from those republics to relocate permanently to areas distant from their cultural communities, western urban areas with an unsatisfied demand for labor recruited temporary labor from Central Asia and used contract workers from Vietnam.[11]

Thus more than a conflict between extensive development and purely demographic factors was producing the crisis. In areas of labor shortage, relief could have been forthcoming by reducing excess demand for labor in existing operations. Yet that exaggerated demand was inherent in the managerial effort to ensure bonus achievement and thus could not be easily reduced without significant restructuring. Further, economic planning that directed resources to such "unproductive" sectors like housing and childcare could have directly influenced low birth rates (as well as reducing the return of migrants from new investment areas like Siberia because of the absence of complementary investment in housing).

Recall, though, our discussion of departmentalism and the gap between planning at the top and concrete decisions below. This suggests that the problem may have been *more* than a failure to integrate "the employment factor" into the formation of the central plan. For example, commenting upon a 1968 report done for the Russian Federation's Gosplan, Lewin wrote:

> In the country's twenty-eight largest towns, construction of new factories was banned. Yet in the current five-year plan, ministries, whether by obtaining exemptions or simply disregarding regulations, had set up enterprises there in order to take advantage of superior infrastructure, causing a serious shortage in those towns.[12]

Four years later, another report on the problem of labor imbalances (including gender imbalances) indicated that the measures taken to rectify the situation had been unsuccessful and attributed the obstacles to "poor planning, a lack of incentives for ministries to locate industries in small towns, instabilities in their plans, and the weakness of their construction capacities."[13]

Was the inability to break with the extensive growth model related to this pattern of the self-orientation of ministries? In his discussion of the sectoral coalitions involving ministries and the enterprises within their spheres, Flaherty concluded that the pattern of investment became "almost entirely a function of sectoral dominance or the heavily skewed correlation of forces existing between the contenders in plan-bargaining." That power was centered in particular in the sectors that had been the beneficiaries of the previous path of extensive development—that is, "an extensive growth coalition." Flaherty proposed that "the evolutionary logic of an extensive accumulation regime" tended toward its own reproduction.[14] In short, changing course to follow a more rational path came up against a problem of "path-dependency"—the existence of existing interests, investments and agendas.[15]

Recall, though, that it was not only the sectoral coalitions that reinforced a pattern of extensive growth. As explained in chapter 3, the social contract itself generated this tendency. Precisely because job rights were an essential aspect of the social contract, expansion of production tended to occur by combining new means of production with workers in new workplaces rather than through introduction of labor-saving technology in existing workplaces. In short, inherent in that social contract that traded security for protagonism on the part of workers was the tendency for extensive rather than intensive growth. This, then, was another potential obstacle to shifting paths.

Accordingly, though in principle there was general agreement that a shift to intensive growth (where increased output and consumption could be supported by increased productivity) was essential, getting there in practice was another matter. There were continual warnings that the Soviet Union could not continue on its existing path. Kosygin was warned by the Academy of Sciences in 1967 in a commissioned report that the economy was lagging behind the United States in all key indicators and that the picture was stark. Subsequently, in 1970, Gosplan's research institute warned that, despite the party's recognition that economic success depended upon intensive growth, all the data pointed in the wrong direction: "Extensive factors are becoming stronger in the development of the Soviet economy, primarily because growth in basic capital assets is outstripping growth in output." This was followed by Gosplan's own 1970 conclusion that "all basic indicators will decelerate, deteriorate or stagnate." Gosplan pointed to a "dual imbalance" on the one hand, between the state's resources and the needs of the national economy; on the other, between the population's monetary income and the output of consumer goods and services.[16]

Despite those warnings, the situation continued to decelerate, deteriorate, and stagnate in the 1970s and 1980s, and the imbalances grew. The situation was summarized in the Report of the CPSU Central Central Committee to the 27th Party Congress delivered by Gorbachev in February 1986, which noted that "difficulties began to build up in the economy in the 1970s, when the rates of growth declined markedly." Even the lower targets of the 9th and 10th five-year plans were not attained; nor was the social program for the period fully carried out despite some important advances. And the reason was that "we had failed to realize the acute and urgent need for converting the economy to intensive methods of development."

Of course, the Central Committee Report continued, "there were many exhortations and a lot of talk on this score, but practically no headway was made." In short, there was stagnation, years of stagnation:

> By inertia, the economy continued to develop largely on an extensive basis, with sights set on drawing additional labour and material resources into production. As a result, the rate of growth of labour productivity and certain other efficiency indicators dropped substantially. The attempts to rectify matters by building new plant affected the problem of balance. The economy, which has enormous resources at its disposal, ran into shortages. A gap appeared between the needs of society and the attained level of production, between the effective demand and the supply of goods.[17]

We need, though, to add something important to this picture of iner-tia and growing crisis. The report indicated that the last quarter-century had been one in which there had been considerable improvement in the standard of living. This was also the observation of Lewin, who wrote that "despite the bad news announced by the planning authorities and clear signs of a system in decline, living standards actually rose during the years of stagnation."[18] Studies indicated that "housing conditions had improved," that "the purchase of consumer durables had increased appreciably," and that the least-well-off had benefited and that there was a reduction of inequality.[19] Further, Flaherty added, the educational lev-els of the working class rose significantly in this period and "most of the progress made by consumers came during the Brezhnev era."[20]

Those advances for workers reflect, of course, the social contract. Indeed, it was precisely those gains that explained, according to Lewin, "the paradox of nostalgia among the population of post-communist Russia for the Brezhnevite 'good old days.'"[21] That social contract, though, was precisely what was threatened by the developing crisis.

WHAT IS TO BE DONE?

Recall the concept of the vanguard presented in chapter 3. Characteristic of the vanguard party is the conviction that the achievement of social-ism will not happen spontaneously and, accordingly, requires leadership. The orchestra needs its conductor: "the interconnection and unity of the process is necessarily represented in a governing will."[22] And the govern-ing will must be the party. As Stalin put it, "The party must stand at the head of the working class."[23]

This self-conception of the party as the necessary conductor on the road to socialism and communism is one that brings with it responsibil-ity and duties. The goal is "the only thing that counts, and no one is more convinced of this than the conductor himself."[24] To *fail* to lead, from this perspective, is to betray its assigned historic role. But what hap-pens when the conductor concludes that the score he has relied upon is flawed—that is, it is not achieving the desired results?

To understand the response of the vanguard party to the signs of emerging crisis, we need to consider both the options and the context. Acceptance of the necessity to turn away from the extensive development model does not point to a single solution. In principle, one way to expand output through productivity gains is by increasing means of production per worker (for example, the substitution of machines for workers). Another is by increasing the efficiency of means of production (that is, expanding output for a given level of means of production). Among methods of doing this would be an increased efficiency of investment, reduction of waste and duplication, and stimulating workers and reducing their alienation. These examples are not mutually exclusive—a combination of these may be particularly effective in increasing productivity.

But remember the context in which the necessity for shifting away from the extensive growth model presents itself. We are not considering a solution in the context of a society where vanguard relations of production alone prevail. Were that the case, the choice of options for the vanguard would be purely technical in nature—that is, identifying the most efficient and immediate method of increasing productivity. However, the crisis in Real Socialism occurred in the context of "contested reproduction"—a struggle between the logic of the vanguard and the logic of capital—and at the center of this struggle was the strengthening or weakening of the vanguard mode of regulation.

Accordingly, the options before the vanguard were political-economic rather than purely technical. They could stress (a) increasing the efficiency of investment through an improved information system and greater investment in machine-building and computerization. This would allow for more coherent planning and greater surveillance of ministries and enterprises and for better plan enforcement. In the short run, this could strengthen the vanguard mode of regulation while moving in the direction of "computopia," the specifically vanguard mode of production.

Alternatively, the vanguard could (b) end particular job rights (the "micro-economic full employment constraint"), encourage enterprise managers to introduce new labor-saving technology, and remove constraints upon managerial initiative in market transactions. In this case, the vanguard would effectively end the social contract by adopting the general perspective of the managers—without, however, relinquishing its own role as conductor of the working class. Finally, the vanguard could (c) focus upon increasing the capacities of workers by breaking down the division between thinking and doing. In this case, it would be moving to end the specific vanguard relation itself by creating the conditions for worker and community democratic management from below.

ARMING THE VANGUARD TECHNICALLY

After the death of Stalin and the drama of the 20th Party Congress in 1956, the political "thaw" associated with Khrushchev created the terrain for new ideas to be advanced for organizing the economy. Among the most important were the proposals to make full use of the potential of computers for economic planning and coordination. Here was the opportunity to work toward the creation of a specifically vanguard mode of production based upon vanguard relations of productions. Writing in 1959 about existing Soviet planning mechanisms, J. M. Montias predicted that if the planners could use successfully the mathematical techniques now available, "they will be tapping a new potential for increased power and growth."[25]

In December 1957, a confidential report from the Soviet Academy of Sciences stressed the gain in efficiency that would result from the use of computers for statistics and planning: "In most cases, such use would make it possible to increase the speed of decision making by hundreds of times and to avoid errors that are currently produced by the unwieldy bureaucratic apparatus involved in these activities." Accordingly, the academy proposed creating a computer center in every region to aid planning, statistics, engineering, and scientific research.[26]

Many steps were taken in this direction. In 1958, the Institute of Electronic Control Machines was established, headed by Isaak Bruk, who two years earlier had proposed creating a hierarchical network of "control machines" to collect, transmit, and process economic data and to facilitate decision making by computer simulation. (In 1961 this institute was placed under the control of the State Economic Research Council, and later the State Planning Committee.) Similarly, in January 1959, engineer Colonel Anatolii Kitov, author of the first Soviet book on digital computers, sent his book to Khrushchev, attaching a letter that advocated "radical change and improvement of methods and means of management by making a transition from the manual and personal forms of management to automated systems, based on the use of electronic computing machines." Computerization of economic management, Kitov argued, would "make it possible to use to the full extent the main economic advantages of the socialist system: planned economy and centralized control. The creation of an automated management system would mean a revolutionary leap in the development of our country and would ensure a complete victory of socialism over capitalism."

Cybernetics in Service of Communism, a volume published in October 1961 on the eve of the 22nd Party Congress by the Council on Cybernetics of the Academy of Science (and annually thereafter) followed the first national conference on mathematical models in economics and planning. In that work, the Soviet economy was interpreted as "a complex cybernetic system, which incorporates an enormous number of various interconnected control loops," and the authors proposed connecting regional computer centers into a nationwide network to create "a single automated system of control of the national economy." And that was precisely the direction contained in the new Party Program adopted at the 22nd Congress, which argued that cybernetics, electronic computers, and control systems "will be widely applied in production processes in manufacturing, the construction industry and transport, in scientific research, in planning and designing, and in accounting and management." Computers, it was declared in the Soviet press, were "machines of communism."[27]

These ideas of "radical change and improvement of methods and means of management" were consistent with the general thrust of Khrushchev's economic measures at the time. Not only did these include enhancing the role of the party relative to state officials (thereby stressing politics in command) and driving down managerial bonuses, but they involved, in particular, replacing ministries with regional economic bodies (*sovnarkhoz*) with the aim of replacing "the massive pyramid of economic ministries (mostly linked to industry), which were overcentralized and oblivious to local interests, and local economic administrative bodies."[28] Indeed, according to Gerovitch, Khrushchev came to look upon cybernetic control as a model of communism: "In our time, the time of the atom, electronics, cybernetics, automation, and assembly lines, what is needed is clarity, ideal coordination and organization of all links in the social system both in material production and in spiritual life." Speaking to intellectuals in 1963, he argued, "Communism is an orderly, organized society. In that society, production will be organized on the basis of automation, cybernetics, and assembly lines."[29]

The possibilities for significant improvement in the quality and execution of central decisions were also apparent to mathematical economists who benefited from the growing interest in economic control. Now, after many years of criticism of mathematical techniques as bourgeois, mathematical economists had an audience. Especially important was the publication in 1959 of Kantorovich's *The Best Use of Economic Resources* (written in 1942 and drawing upon his earlier development of linear programming in 1939). This work pointed to the problem of making decisions based upon a price structure that did not take into account the real cost of bringing new resources into use, and it was the basis for an argument that the existing prices assigned to particular activities distorted rational economic decision making, generating waste and excess costs.

Although critical of the existing methods of calculation, that argument was not a challenge to the process of planning or vanguard relations itself. On the contrary, general objectives were to be given from above, and the point was to find the most efficient means of achieving those goals. Mathematical methods, Kantorovich argued, were especially useful for finding concrete solutions for a socialist economy and for discovering "the advantages of this highly perfected social structure." Socialist society, he stressed, was "by its nature, capable of securing a more complete and rational use of productive resources." Accordingly, "for each sector of socialist production and for socialist society as a whole, an optimal plan has a concrete reality."[30]

There can be little doubt those at the top hoped that "improved flows of information and better communications could be achieved with the help of computers and systems analysis so as to enable them to maintain the prevailing highly centralized management without basic alterations in the position of the lower echelons."[31] Thus, in 1962, they supported the proposal of Viktor Glushkov, director of the Institute of Cybernetics, to build "an automated system for economic planning and management on the basis of a nationwide computer network." Working closely with Nikolai Federenko, head of the Central Economic Mathematical Institute, the two published a joint article calling for a unified system of optimal planning and management in 1964, proposing that this would provide support for "optimal decision-making on a national scale." It called for a major network of computer centers, with all economic data collected and stored in data centers and available to all relevant agencies. Consistent with Khrushchev's overhaul of the ministries at this time, Glushhov's proposal called for significant oversight over bureaucrats within the economic sphere, creating "detailed lists of their duties, to determine clearly the order of document processing, the chain of responsibility, the timetable, and so on."[32]

Not surprisingly, Glushkov's proposal for computerization worried managers and bureaucrats because it "ultimately threatened to make them redundant." But it also was opposed by economists who viewed it "as a conservative attempt to further centralize the control of the economy and to suppress the autonomy of small economic units." For them, "Glushkov's project merely conserved obsolete forms of centralized economic management." His proposal was presented formally to the government in June 1964; in October, however, Khrushchev was ousted. Accordingly, when Glushkov's project came up for consideration in November before the new government headed by Brezhnev and Kosygin, the balance of forces was no longer as favorable and the opposition succeeded in stalling any development of a national network. [33]

The thrust now (in addition to the dismantling of Khrushchev's regional economic councils and restoration of the power of the ministries) was to expand the economic independence of enterprises by reducing the number of their success indicators and allowing them to retain more resources for individual investments. Kosygin stressed increasing material incentive for the managers and for the workers: "It is necessary to introduce a system under which the enterprise's opportunities for improving the remuneration of its workers would be determined, above all, by the growth of production, improved quality, increased profits and greater profitability of production."[34]

Without question, this emphasis upon increasing the power of the enterprises introduced a different theme. Though it didn't mean an end to the focus upon computerization and optimal planning, it did raise questions about priorities. Concerned about this question, Novozhilov, a leading mathematical economist, wrote in 1966: "It is easy to extend the rights of the enterprise. It is difficult, however, as a result of this extension to reconcile the interests of the enterprise employees with those of the economy." *First*, you had to develop a rational set of prices and planning. Accordingly, the expansion of enterprise powers should be "the last link in the tendency to develop a system of managing a socialist economy," and it should be developed on the basis of the optimization of planning and price setting. Novozhilov insisted that "the optimization of planning is the leading link in the chain." Thus the implementation of "the profound transformation of industrial management" envisioned could only be "gradual." "At the present moment," he argued, "the planning of prices is the main bottleneck in the organization of the socialist economy."[35]

In the late 1960s and 1970s, there was continued stress upon the importance of cybernetics and computerization for the economy. Linear programming techniques were increasingly utilized for examining particular projects, resolutions were passed (including support for Glushkov's subsequent watered-down proposals for a national information system), and Federenko's institute received substantial support. But in the balancing act between reforms at the level of enterprise management and measures strengthening the vanguard mode of regulation, the advantages of neither could be realized. Indeed, the interaction between the two logics produced impasse.

Despite the steps begun in 1966 toward enterprise independence, within a short time it was clear to supporters like Nove that "the old system, whether of ideas or organizational-economic substance, has survived without fundamental change."[36] Those opposed to market reforms were looking to "computerized management, and improved information flow" in order to "improve economic performance without endangering the *status quo*."[37] And they were successful at this point in checking the reform measures. As Nove complained, "The power to allocate resources and to take production decisions remains with the central authorities."[38]

And yet the momentum for the creation of a national network that could help to plan the economy as a single factory was lost. Indeed, the idea of creating a network of computer centers was attacked as far too costly—with one reform economist (Popov) describing it as a plan to construct pyramids across the country. In the absence of a political commitment to create that unified network, the vacuum was filled as individual ministries and institutions built their own computer systems and developed their own information systems. And those systems were incompatible. Gerovitch pointed out that "by accelerating the development of branch-based incompatible systems, the ministries effectively blocked the idea of a national computer network." [39]

The initial hopes for computerization as a solution faded. One report from 1985 indicated that the results from the introduction of computers were "only a quarter or a fifth as effective as had been hoped."[40] The effect was that by the 1980s there was "widespread skepticism" about the usefulness of management information and control systems. According to economist Michael Ellman, "This largely resulted from the failure to fulfil the earlier exaggerated hopes about the returns to be obtained from their introduction in the economy."[41] The problems for which this was to be a solution, though, were not disappearing; indeed, they were increasing. So where could the conductor turn?

The Class Perspective of the Economists

Ideas can be a material force when they seize the minds of the vanguard. And, in the Battle of Ideas, the constrained capitalists had strong weapons. They had economists as their ideological representatives. Those economists were not themselves would-be capitalists or necessarily conscious representatives of capital. However, as Marx commented about the spokespersons of the petit bourgeoisie:

> What makes them representatives of the petty bourgeoisie is the fact that in their minds they do not get beyond the limits which the latter do not get beyond in life, that they are consequently driven, theoretically, to the same problems and solutions to which material interest and social position drive the latter practically.[42]

In this case, too, the economists tended to be stuck within class limits. In particular, their blind spot was the working class. The alternative they offered to the hierarchical rule of the vanguard did not challenge the domination of workers within the workplace and society. Instead, the economists stressed the constraints upon the managers. They did not talk about dynamic inefficiency as the effect of the separation of thinking and doing upon the capacities of workers. Instead, the economists began and ended with the inefficiencies that managers confronted on a daily basis as the result of their domination from above.

"Free the manager" was their solution. Of course, they did not openly identify the interests of the managers as the goal. Rather, Lewin sympathetically noted that "economists discovered the forgotten person, the consumer" and insisted that production and economic activity should "serve consumers." Responding to the consumer, they asserted, was "the very necessity of progress."[43] In advocating an end to everything that constrained the manager, the economists argued that "the *special* conditions of its emancipation are the *general* conditions within the frame of which alone modern society can be saved."[44]

But saved from what? Saved on the one hand from the exercise of property rights by the vanguard. Saved on the other hand from the social contract that prevented the managers from exercising power over workers. Saved *in general* from the dysfunctions of the Soviet economy for which the only solution was to free the managers. In contrast to the managers themselves (affected in their everyday activity by their relations with the logic of the vanguard), the economists represent the logic of capital in its purity.

In their search for the general conditions for saving Soviet society, the economists began with a focus upon abstract efficiency: *the firm is too large.* By insisting upon treating the economy as "one factory" run from one center, they argued, the central planners have created extensive inefficiency. All problems, indeed, could be traced back to overcentralization. Central planning "had to bear the brunt as mainspring of all the dysfunctions." Considering "every side of the planners' work—the techniques involved in doing the job, fixing the targets, and getting results from subordinates," economists concluded that "the existing degree of centralization was in itself dysfunctional and untenable."[45]

Accordingly, the answer was to reduce the size of the firm—to move away from the "heavy concentration of decisions at the hungry and power-greedy center, which was flooded with information that it could not properly digest and so tended to lose touch with reality."[46] The answer was to move away from "hierarchically vertical command lines" and to recognize that "horizontal contacts are indispensable for an optimally functioning economy."[47] "Horizontal," though, did not mean local planning and conscious coordination from below. Horizontal meant markets. There was "widespread acceptance" among the economists, Lewin argued, that "market categories are not alien to socialism but inherent to it."[48]

But why *inherent?* Because, it was claimed, the enterprises were separate and had separate interests. "Writers pointed out that the economy was composed of thousands of producing units, enterprises and factories that were relatively independent, quite distinctly separated from others." And since the "producers could not appropriate products without selling their own in exchange," they were producing "commodities" rather than "products." So according to Lewin, "The majority of Soviet economists yielded to evidence and accepted that, in all its sectors, the Soviet economy was and is a commodity producer." There was, he declared, "enough proof" that "on the whole the products were exchanged and not just directly appropriated and distributed." In short, rather than being replaced by planning, the market was there and had "proved to be a vitally important mechanism of the socialist economy."[49]

Preventing these economically independent enterprises from functioning in the market by imposing vertical command lines, from this perspective, was to substitute voluntarism for real economic relations—a voluntarism, too, that could not possibly be successful because the state had neither the knowledge nor capability for administrative-command planning. Imposing this, Nemchinov argued, was "contrary to the contemporary conditions of the complex and deep division of social labor that characterizes all the spheres of the socialist national economy."[50] The result, he wrote in 1965, was an economic system "fettered from top to bottom"; what existed was "an ossified, mechanical system in which all the directing parameters were given in advance and the whole system was fettered from top to bottom, in any given moment, and at any given point."[51]

So, what was to be done? The answer was not to end planning as such. Medium- and long-term plans and forecasts remained essential, but the annual plan, the *operational plan* with its detailed targets and directions from above, had to be replaced by "economic levers," incentives that would guide individual enterprises to act in society's interest by following their own interest. "The consensus among reformers," Lewin commented, "seemed to be that central planning should concentrate on long-term macroeconomic objectives" while at the microeconomic level the enterprise "in its everyday activity . . . would be left free to work for the consumer rather than for the plan."[52]

Indeed, as noted above, shifting initiative to the enterprises was the stated goal of the economic reform introduced after the removal of Khrushchev. The first clause of the Statute of the Socialist Industrial Enterprise approved in October 1965 read: "The socialist industrial enterprise shall be the basic unit of the national economy in the U.S.S.R. Its operation shall be based on centralized direction combined with economic independence and initiative on the part of the enterprise."[53] Of course, a shift from considering the economy as a whole to making individual enterprises the basic units of the economy involved more than just a focus upon efficiency. Although the argument against central planning took the form of a critique of inefficiency, it must not be considered abstractly—that is, outside the concrete class struggle that was occurring.

Rather, we need to understand these arguments in the context of the struggle between the logic of the vanguard and the logic of capital.

Recall Bettelheim's question. Is the state able to subordinate those who possess the means of production, the enterprise managers? The state, he proposed, acts as proprietor of the means of production possessed by the enterprises when "these means are directly brought under control and put into operation," and this occurs through the "*plan* and the planned relations that are derived from this plan." To yield to the enterprises the power to make decisions about their use of the means of production they possess, from this perspective, was to transfer property rights to those enterprises.[54]

The economic reformers argued, however, that the state in fact did not have the power to direct the economy; it only had the power to *interfere with enterprises*; that is, there were objective limits to the state's ability to exercise its property rights. Shkredov wrote in 1967 that "the scope of planning was excessive because the juridical socialization of the means and products did not coincide with economic socialization."[55] Accordingly, "inept interference in the economy by the state and its arbitrariness had to be eliminated."[56]

It was a familiar Marxist argument: the productive forces have come into conflict with the relations of production that have changed from forms of development of the productive forces into their fetters; that is, the Soviet economy was the victim of its own success. In the past, the economists conceded, administrative-command methods had industrialized and developed the productive forces of the Soviet Union. Centralized control of the economy can be successful, Maurice Dobb proposed, when the situation makes "policy objectives relatively simple" and when the structure of the economy is "relatively simple rather than complex."[57] But those methods were no longer appropriate: the very success of the model had created a complex economy in which administrative-command was positively harmful to the economy.

The failure to adjust the pattern of property rights to the real productive relations in the economy meant for Shkredov that "the economy was torn asunder by a basic contradiction between the regulatory function of the proprietor-state and the laws of the market economy."[58] The general conclusion of reformers was that "The inadequate 'production relations' hampering economic development must be adapted to the 'productive forces,' otherwise crises developed." However, the existing system itself "did not have the capacity to 'readapt' [*perestroit'sia*] to reorganize planning and management institutions so that they would match the new conditions."[59] Therefore, it was essential to change the relations of production so they could be forms of development of productive forces once again. Insofar as producing units were economically separate, property rights should be exercised by the real possessors—the enterprises.[60]

That was precisely what supporters of the existing system of central planning rejected. They rejected the idea of abandoning the annual plan with its specific directives for enterprises and rejected the proposal to move toward markets. In 1968, for example, the head of the Prices Committee opposed "the abandonment of compulsory quantitative indicators" and argued that market prices are "alien to our economy and contradict the task of centralized planning." The balance between demand and supply, Sitnin insisted, "is the task of the planning organs."[61]

Further, it was a distortion, a substitution of a wish for reality, to say (as Lewin did) that "the majority of Soviet economists yielded to evidence and accepted that, in all its sectors, the Soviet economy was and is a commodity producer." How could it be said that the enterprises had separate interests and that they produced "commodities" rather than "products" when those enterprises were subordinated to the plan that assigned them input sources and output channels and where they did not demand a quid pro quo for distributing their output? Lopatkin (predictably described by Lewin as "dogmatic") stressed that the enterprise was subordinate to the state: "The socialist enterprise does not and cannot have any distinct interests of its own, analogous to the interests of a private entrepreneur." Society had created the enterprise and it was "free to liquidate it, not to speak about preempting resources from it."[62]

Precisely because of strong opposition, the reformers were not successful at this point in advancing the program announced in 1965, and those reforms themselves were scaled back within a few years. Thus impasse (another one!) marked by that "basic contradiction between the regulatory function of the proprietor-state and the laws of the market economy;" that is, that contested reproduction in which the law of command and the law of value interacted. It was not until the early 1980s (and the death of Brezhnev) that those advocating managerial independence were emboldened to resume the offensive.

Again, the effect of lagging relations of production upon the productive forces was posed explicitly. "Every important step in the development of the productive forces of socialism requires the correction in the improvement of this whole real system of socialist productive production relations," Butenko wrote in 1982. Similarly, Tatiana Zalavskaia argued in the "Novosibirsk Report" in 1983 that productive relations had fallen considerably behind the level of development of productive forces. You could not reform those relations, however, through a *piecemeal* approach because a set of relations of production constitutes an integrated system, a whole. Therefore, only a "profound restructuring [*perestroika*]" can succeed, one that substitutes for the old a "new economic mechanism"—in short, a new set of productive relations, a new whole.[63]

This call for "perestroika" was increasingly answered. For example, in 1983, on the hundredth anniversary of Marx's death, Andropov (the new general secretary of the party) wrote that "our work directed at the improvement and restructuring [*perestroika*] of the economic mechanism, of forms and methods of management has lagged behind the demands posed by the achieved level of material-technical, social, and intellectual development of Soviet society," and he called explicitly for change in the "forms of the organization of economic life" in order to "accelerate the progress of the productive forces." That, too, was the theme of the new program adopted at the 27th Party Congress under Gorbachev in 1986: it referred to the "mistakes of the seventies and early eighties" and stressed the necessity for "the constant improvement of production relations" to correspond with "dynamically developing productive forces."[64]

This, of course, was the theme of Gorbachev's own report to the 27th Congress. "We cannot limit ourselves to partial improvements. A radical reform is needed." This involved a significant theoretical shift: "Life prompts us to take a new look at some theoretical ideas and concepts." In particular, Gorbachev continued, "practice has revealed the insolvency of the ideas that under the conditions of socialism *the conformity of production relations to the nature of the productive forces* is ensured automatically." The relations of production had to be improved and "outdated economic management methods" had to be replaced by new ones. One important aspect called for "resolutely enlarging the framework of the autonomy of associations and enterprises." Indeed, Gorbachev underlined its importance by stressing that "everything we are doing to improve management and planning and to readjust organizational structures is aimed at creating the conditions for *effective functioning of the basic link of the economic system: the association or enterprise.*"[65]

The program of perestroika thus meant that the managers would be successful in wresting clear property rights over the enterprises from the vanguard. But acceptance of the enterprises as the "basic unit" of the economy was only one part of the struggle to free the managers. As long as workers continued to be protected through the social contract, part of the old system would still be present. How successful would market reforms be under this constraint? The other aspect of the Battle of Ideas for the managers and their ideological representatives was the necessity to attack the social contract. In short, the second side of the Battle of Ideas for the economists was the assault on the working class.

Although Gavriil Popov proposed in 1980 to "limit the right to work" in order to allow greater managerial flexibility, few were prepared to take this step initially.[66] The assault on this front, however, increased as the crisis of the economy deepened and the push to transfer all property rights to the enterprise managers intensified. Now the problem facing the economy was identified as what G. Lisichkin called in 1987 an "archaic leveling consciousness" that predominated among the bulk of a working class "enfeebled by a long-term dependence" on a collectivist social welfare state. The economic reformers concluded that it was necessary to dismantle a system of "enervating *Garantirovannost*" [literally Guarantedness or the guarantee of a wide range of socioeconomic entitlements]. Excessive welfare entitlements, argued Zaslavskaia, led to the "slackening of administrative and economic compulsion for energetic labor in social production," and it was time to reduce significantly the social wage and to restore a "personal interest in hard efficient labor."[67]

As part of this attack on the social contract, the reformers proposed commodification of social services—for example, establishment of a two-tier public and private health care system.[68] Also, they called for ending all food subsidies and allowing prices to be determined by the market.[69] Driving down the real wages of what reformers viewed as "a privileged social constituency of the Brezhnevian social contract" was all part of this Soviet version of neoliberalism. And then there was the attack on the property rights of workers—their job rights.

"Socialism is not philanthropy automatically guaranteeing everyone employment irrespective of his or her ability to do the job," argued Stanislav Shatalin in 1986. Subsequently chosen by Gorbachev to prepare his 500-Day Plan for reforming the Soviet economy, he certainly was not alone in the attack on job rights. Sounding like a champion of Thatcher and Reagan, Nikolai Shmeliov complained about the "economic damage caused by a parasitic confidence in guaranteed jobs," and he urged the government to consider the advantages that a "comparatively small reserve army of labor" could bring to a socialist political economy. "Excessive full employment" produced "a host of social ills," and "the real danger of losing a job . . . is a good cure for laziness, drunkenness and irresponsibility."[70]

Given the sensitivity of this question, an explicit attack on job rights was not introduced as part of the perestroika project; however, the shift that stressed the independence and initiative of the enterprises, calling upon them to generate their funds internally through "cost-accounting" (*khozraschet*), effectively meant that the managers were given the green light to lay off redundant workers. Thus, even though all the goals of the economic reformers were not achieved immediately (especially because of continuing resistance among supporters of vanguard relations), the trajectory was clear—the end to the mode of regulation characterized by the social contract.

But why? Given that the position advanced by the economists was a class perspective that challenged vanguard relations and attacked the working class (which the vanguard had supported with the social contract), why did the vanguard accept the position of the constrained capitalists, the enterprise managers?

The Vanguard Party in the Context
of Contested Reproduction

In part, the decision of the vanguard reflected the Battle of Ideas. The economists, after all, had "science" behind them—the science of mainstream Western (that is, neoclassical) economics.[71] But this was not a decision made in abstraction. The choice was not made by a vanguard party in its "purity," (as discussed in chapter 3) but rather by one "infected in the course of its interaction with other elements (both contingent and inherent)." In short, rather than the abstract concept of the vanguard, here we must deal with the concrete vanguard—the vanguard that emerged in the context of contested reproduction.

This was not, after all, a society consisting only of vanguard relations of production but one that contained as well the logic of capital as manifested in the behavior of the managers. Thus the vanguard party was predictably deformed, more or less, by its interaction with that other logic. For one, the self-oriented managers, who had been permitted to possess the state-owned means of production, tended to be individual members of the vanguard party. In short, the conflict between the logic of the vanguard and the logic of capital was not something outside the vanguard party but was internalized.

Yet the effect of the logic of capital upon the vanguard party went well beyond the actual number of managers who were party members. The social contract always included material self-interest for the working class; however, the substitution of managers actively engaged in maximizing their own income in place of managers "guided by noble purposes who work long, hard hours in the firm belief that in doing so they serve the cause of their party and of the people, the common good and the interests of mankind" has a predictable influence.[72]

Existing members who retain their "belief in the party's ideas, agreement with the official ideology, and enthusiasm for the plan's objectives" cannot help but be affected.[73] Seeing the acceptability of income-maximizing behavior and the ability of managers to advance within the state and party increases the ability of party members to rationalize their own access to special advantages like higher incomes, access to scarce goods, better medical and recreational facilities. Further, bureaucrats charged with direct supervision of enterprise managers, in addition to becoming reliant upon the latter for plan fulfillment, can become beneficiaries of their monetary support. In this way, lobbies and sectoral coalitions form and increasingly usurp the authority of the "nominally sovereign central agencies."[74]

These are conditions in which members of the vanguard act less as the vanguard "personified" and come to focus increasingly upon privileges associated with positions in the hierarchy. The "second soul" dwelling within the breast of the member of the vanguard, with its focus upon the accumulation of pleasures, is less and less subordinated (or repressed) by the logic of the vanguard. In this situation, while the vanguard party may continue to attract the best in the society, it may also get the worst. The tendency to seek party membership (and to simulate the appropriate behavior) may be increasingly based upon the potential for career advancement and securing special advantages. As one specialist in the USSR told Alena Ledeneva, "It was common knowledge that unless one was a party member, he or she could not be appointed for a leading position. Party membership was like an extra diploma to qualify for further career opportunities."[75] The disease spreads throughout the party—affecting both existing members and new recruits.

This party (and not the "pure" one), a party that contains within it that "contradiction between the regulatory function of the proprietor-state and the laws of the market economy," is the one that chooses what is to be done in the face of economic crisis. Contested reproduction within the vanguard party itself produces an impasse in which the adherents of vanguard relations increasingly lose confidence in the previous path and those who support capitalist relations are increasingly emboldened.

Capital ultimately won the Battle of Ideas in the Soviet Union because it successfully invaded the vanguard party. But capital could not win the struggle of contested reproduction by itself. To advance in Real Socialism, "the rising bourgeoisie needs the power of the state"— the *vanguard* state. Subordination of the logic of the vanguard and the expanded reproduction of capitalist relations of production was made possible by the vanguard's own mode of regulation.

6—From Moral Economy to Political Economy

But what about the ideas of the working class in this Battle of Ideas? Who articulated those ideas within Real Socialism? The answer is predictable. Characteristic of the vanguard relation is that the *vanguard* speaks on behalf of the working class. Any attempts by workers to organize independently of the official channels appointed by the vanguard to represent them were repressed. Without space for autonomous organization or, indeed, effective communication among themselves, workers in the Soviet Union were disarmed in the ideological struggle.

The working class was disarmed in another way: rather than a Marxism that places at its center the "key link" of human development and practice, on offer was Vanguard Marxism, a deformation similar to vanguard state ownership and vanguard planning. Rather than stressing the worker and community decision making that builds the capacities of workers, Vanguard Marxism was the ideological counterpart of the various vanguard transmission belts (like official trade unions) from the conductor to the working class which were, in practice, weapons against the working class.

Nevertheless, despite the extent to which Vanguard Marxism disarmed the working class in the ideological struggle, this does not mean workers had no ideas. However, it is important not to project the goals of an Abstract Proletariat upon the real working class produced within Real Socialism. Substituting wishes for concrete circumstances is a very familiar problem.

THE NORMS OF THE WORKING CLASS IN REAL SOCIALISM

In the period under consideration, workers in Real Socialism expected the social contract to be honored. In return for acquiescing to their absence of power within the workplace and society, they considered themselves entitled to security and improving conditions of life. Part of that was obtained through their job rights and the absence of a reserve army of labor as well as the full employment economy that allowed them to both minimize the length and intensity of their workday and to increase their income by changing jobs. But also important was the existence of fixed prices for necessities that allowed rising income to be transformed into rising consumption.

What if the vanguard failed to deliver on its side? In chapter 2 we saw that the vanguard was worried that violation of existing norms "sooner or later entails serious political and social consequences, tensions and even shocks."[1] Precisely for this reason, planners attempted during this period to satisfy the expectations and sense of entitlement of the working class. In the relation between vanguard and working class as embodied in the social contract, "there was a system of mutual obligations."[2]

As well as the social norms concerning the obligation of the vanguard to workers, the conceptions of right and wrong characteristic of relations among workers in Real Socialism were also essential to understand. These relations were not independent of the specific relation of workers to the means of production—in particular, their property rights as embodied in the real existence of job rights (and reinforced ideologically by the concept of a workers' state). Given the chronic shortages of necessities, that perception of property rights (however ill-defined) provided rationalization for informal ways of obtaining goods and services—in particular, theft.[3]

Insofar as one's workplace provides access to scarce material resources, it was viewed as acceptable behavior for individuals (as individuals) to draw upon those resources and to make them available to friends, neighbors, members of one's social network, and for the purpose of exchange for desired goods (that is, within a second economy). Ledeneva comments, "In a state-controlled economy of the Soviet type, state property was omnipresent, and every working citizen was in direct contact with it at her/his place of work. Most reliable sources agree that theft of socialist (state) property was almost as widespread as state property itself."[4]

Some theft served as a means for workers to supplement their official incomes through diverted materials for the purpose of exchange or for second jobs (which often involved the private use of means of production from their workplace). However, more was involved in theft than simply increasing one's income. Under conditions of shortages, providing scarce supplies to friends and acquaintances gave one great satisfaction: "To bring something from the workplace became a norm and even a matter of pride if something was given to a friend in trouble or in need."[5] This, indeed, was one of the meanings of the Russian term *blat,* which distinguished it in the minds of people from theft as such: "To obtain something by *blat*—in modest volume, with discretion, normally in situations of urgent need and within a closed personal circle—is a norm; to exceed limits is theft, corruption, etc."[6]

Indeed, Ledeneva comments about these relations among people that they "felt very comfortable about smuggling things or fiddling (it was collective, i.e. partly their property after all!) for their friends but hated the idea of tradespeople or cadres doing the same."[7] In these relations, "sharing access with friends and acquaintances became so routine that the difference between *blat* and friendly relations became blurred: one almost became consequent upon the other."[8] Similar to gift exchange, she proposed that *blat* "underwrites social relations and is concerned with social reproduction." Indeed, it builds upon social relations that already exist, and the reciprocity in those relations is "created and preserved by a mutual sense of 'fairness' and trust."[9]

But *blat* relations and their counterparts elsewhere in Real Socialism were not isolated phenomena. Consider the difficulties in getting workers fired even for blatant alcoholism and the social acceptability of theft from the workplace. There was a popular consensus that everyone should be able to satisfy their basic needs (reflected in *blat*), a conception of an egalitarian society and a belief in the importance of the reduction of insecurity (and thus in employment and income).

THE MORAL ECONOMY OF THE WORKING CLASS

All this was part of a set of social norms and beliefs as to right and wrong, which, taken together, we may designate as the "moral economy" of the working class in Real Socialism. This concept (and, indeed, the wording itself) comes from what E. P. Thompson called "the moral economy of the poor" in his classic article, "The Moral Economy of the English Crowd in the Eighteenth Century."[10] The food riots of this period, he argued, reflected a broad and passionate consensus on what was right, leading to a sharp reaction to egregious violations of that conception of justice. Commenting on Thompson's account, Li Jun observed, "Rioters were legitimized by the belief that they were defending traditional rights or customs that were supported by the wider consensus of the community."[11]

Similarly, in his work on "the moral economy of the peasant," James Scott focused upon the notion of economic justice among peasants and pointed to the revolts and rebellions that could erupt when those notions were violated. For Scott, these conceptions of justice had their roots in the need for maintaining subsistence. Indeed, an overriding focus upon subsistence characterized relations both among peasants and between peasants and those who exploited them.[12] "The test for the peasant," Scott proposed, "is more likely to be 'What is left?' than 'How much is taken?' "[13]

From this perspective, exploitation as such is not sufficient to generate riots, revolts, and rebellions. "Moral economists," Kopstein commented in his study of worker resistance in East Germany, "posit the existence of a tacit social contract in almost every long-standing social formation in which subaltern groups tolerate their own exploitation." They tolerate that exploitation as long as they are left enough for themselves—that is, are able to secure their expected subsistence. When the prevailing norm is violated, however, Kopstein proposed that it generates "resistance ranging from shirking, grumbling, foot dragging, false compliance, dissimulation, and other 'weapons of the weak,' to open strikes and other forms of collective action." But only to *negate* that violation. According to moral economists, Kopstein reported, "exploited groups simply want to restore their previous standards before the downturn. Rarely do they try to overturn the existing order altogether."[14]

The underlying concept here is one of an *equilibrium*—a concept that Thompson employed explicitly in talking about "a particular set of social relations, a particular equilibrium between paternalist authority and the crowd."[15] When that equilibrium is disturbed, there is a feedback mechanism: masses (peasants, crowd, workers) react to restore the conditions corresponding to the social norms supported by the consensus of the community. Thus, all other things equal, a tendency toward stability. The begged question, though, is what was the *source* of those norms?

For Thompson, Scott, and other developers of the concept of moral economy, the reference point revolved around the need for subsistence in traditional peasant society—both before the advance of the political economy of capital and in defensive struggle against it. Was peasant society, then, the source of the moral economy in Real Socialism? Were the social norms of workers inherited from the moral economy of peasants—and thus a characteristic that must be overcome in a process of modernization?

Certainly, for the economic reformers who supported the removal of constraints upon managers, the elements of the moral economy (and, in particular, the notion of egalitarian relations) all looked *backward*—to traditional peasant society. Lisichkin, for example, described what we have called the moral economy of the working class in Real Socialism as the continuation of an "archaic leveling consciousness" and a "feudal" egalitarian normative matrix.[16] Similarly, the Yugoslav sociologist Josip Zupanov proposed that the "egalitarian syndrome" was a "relic of traditional societies"—indeed, their "vicious legacy."[17]

Traditional social norms and beliefs that valued equality—this was the enemy to be combated! Those retained elements of traditional peasant culture, according to neoliberal advisors of Gorbachev, were at the root of the resistance to change: they had produced a "society contaminated by an egalitarian psychology" that rejected "all manifestations of individualism, independence, personal initiative, and the successes which are bound up with this."[18] Zupanov made the same point: the egalitarian syndrome, with its "fear of private [individual] initiative, anti-professionalism, intellectual levelling-down and anti-intellectualism," was a critical obstacle toward the development of a modern industrial society.[19]

Indeed, if these legacies of traditional peasant culture were acting as fetters upon the development of productive forces, then it followed that they must be recognized as distinctly "non-proletarian." "Marxism-Leninism decisively sweeps away the petty-bourgeois theory of levelling distribution and consumption," declared Efim Manevich, a Soviet labor economist in 1985. "Levelling," he argued, "is incompatible with the interests of the development of socialist production." Indeed, such ideas about universal equality, he explained, are "alien to the proletariat."[20]

There is a problem in such assertions. Given their incorporation within the social contract, how alien to the existing (as opposed to the theoretical) proletariat could such ideas be? In fact, the social contract in Real Socialism reinforced and *validated* the moral economy of the working class. It ensured that the concept of justice of workers received support. Though that social contract did not exclude exploitation, it did yield something workers wanted. Kopstein argued, for example, that "along with job security, East German workers had the power to demand a rough-and-ready sort of wage egalitarianism and consumer prices that remained low relative to wages."[21]

And the same argument for a moral economy of the working class and the support that the social contract provided is explicit in Li Jun's examination of strikes in China: "Simply put, in the Chinese socialist setting, workers view themselves as having a relationship with the state, a relationship which operates according to the norm of reciprocity: the state is expected to have committed itself to ensuring that the workers have a decent living by providing job security and a prodigious welfare package, while workers, in return, advocate the party ruling by giving their political support and loyalty to the state." To support what Li Jun calls "the workers' moral economy," it was expected that the state authority would fulfill "its responsibility to protect and benefit its working class in the form of the 'iron rice bowl.'"[22]

In short, the moral economy of the working class in Real Socialism was *not* simply the inheritance of traditional peasant society. Essential to its existence was a combination, a combination in which the role of the vanguard was critical. Acknowledging this central point, Zupanov described the egalitarian syndrome as a "fusion." It was, he argued, "basically composed of two sets of complementary value orientations and attitudes—of egalitarian and authoritative ones." In this combination, the orientation toward egalitarianism was "inextricably linked to the support for an authoritative state which was supposed to take care of egalitarian expectations."[23] Thus the egalitarian syndrome legitimized the position of the vanguard: "It provided a basis for a stable interaction between the socialist political elite and the strategic parts of the population, especially manual workers."[24]

According to Zupanov, this particular fusion provided a mass basis for "statism." The point was made as well by Alex Pravda in 1981:

> What anchors most Soviet and East European workers' attachment to "real existing socialism" is full employment, a welfare wage, low income differentials and stable food prices. In a sense workers' acceptance of strong state control is conditioned by that state's delivery of the above package of security-welfare benefits. The situation may be seen as a tacit social compact which underpins the relationship between workers and regime in all industrialised Communist states.[25]

For the reformers, though, the "equilibrium" supported by this compact was, rather, one of *stagnation*. That fusion prevented the development of what the Polish sociologist P. Sztompka called "civilisational competence . . . a complex set of rules, norms and values, habits and reflexes, codes and matrixes, blueprints and formats" whose components are "enterprise, civic, discursive and everyday culture." Sztompka argued that "the decades of Real Socialism not only blocked the appearance of civilisational competence, but in many ways helped to shape [a] contrary cultural syndrome—civilisational incompetence."[26] This cultural incompetence, he proposed, was mostly a result of the "socialist elite's indoctrination of and control over [the] population."

In short, the ideological claim of the existence of a workers' state and the real support for the aspirations of workers provided through the social contract were important sources for the moral economy of the working class. In the case of the major strike movement (triggered by price increases) in Novocherkassk in the Soviet Union in 1962, Mandel reported that the working-class consciousness "came from the workers' schooling, from books and films and, of course, from their shared situation."[27] That leaders constantly stressed their commitment to socialism, too, had clear consequences. "From the official ideology of Marxism-Leninism, to which they are generally indifferent," Pravda commented, "workers have 'salvaged' notions of security, welfare and equality, and see full employment, a welfare wage, low income differentials and stable prices as basic socialist rights."[28]

Thus, although elements from traditional peasant societies were present, parts do not exist outside particular wholes. We need to consider the ideas of workers as they were reproduced within this new whole. Rather than being challenged by what Thompson called a new political economy "disinfested of intrusive moral imperatives," the norms associated with the moral economy were strengthened and deepened within "Real Socialism." Tendencies toward equality and low income differences, for example, were reinforced in the Soviet Union through what Gorbachev subsequently called "serious infractions of the socialist principle of distribution according to work." The result, the Soviet leader argued, was that "a mentality of dependence has developed. In people's consciousness, the psychology of levelling has taken root."[29] Such ideas were more than an inheritance from traditional society—they were produced and reproduced within the new context.

However, as in the case of Thompson's consideration of the moral economy of the eighteenth-century crowd, the ideas of workers not only incorporated but also transcended vanguard relations as embodied in the social contract. Although "the crowd derived its sense of legitimation, in fact, from the paternalist model"—and re-echoed such notions "so loudly in their turn that the authorities were, in some measure, the prisoners of the people"—in its support for direct action by the crowd "the moral economy of the crowd broke decisively with that of the paternalists."[30] Similarly, the moral economy of the working class in Real Socialism broke decisively with the perspective of the vanguard with respect to the popular consensus about theft by individuals. Workers "felt very comfortable," as noted above, at smuggling things from work for their friends, given that this state property "was collective, i.e. partly their property after all!"[31]

There was, however, a *general* gap between the proclamations of those at the top and the ideas of workers. "Compelled to participate in rituals that proclaimed socialism to be just, efficient and egalitarian," Burawoy observed with respect to workers, "they were only too keenly aware of the injustices, inefficiencies and inequalities that pervaded their lives." In this respect, the system was vulnerable to an "immanent critique, demanding that the system live up to its promises."[32]

In the absence of their specific articulation and development, could the ideas of workers be other than the basis for defensive responses—much like peasant responses to violations of their social norms? "The typical moral economy rebellion or strike," Kopstein indicated, "is spontaneous, leaderless and defensive."[33] Where workers do not proceed beyond moral economy on the basis of a conscious alternative, Burawoy proposed a possible result: "Immanent critique, calling attention to the failed promises of socialism, can lead to cynicism and retreat if it is not attached to social movements inspired by alternatives struggling to free themselves from within the girders of the existent. That is what happened."[34]

As we have seen, though, more than this happened as the result of the disarming of workers in Real Socialism. The moral economy of the working class itself was assaulted as the political economy of capital advanced. Now, in Thompson's words, "the 'nature of things' which had once made imperative, in times of dearth, at least some symbolic solidarity between the rulers and the poor, now dictated solidarity between the rulers and 'the Employment of Capital.'"[35] In Real Socialism, the apparent social contract came to an end.

BEYOND MORAL ECONOMY

If workers struggle over the ideas and norms associated with moral economy, then clearly those ideas are a material force. By considering those
social norms and beliefs as to what is right and what is wrong, we can
root our analysis in the concrete and avoid the tendency to begin with
a preconceived theory and then search for concrete support to serve as
footnotes to the theory.[36] Further, we also may be able to point to elements in the moral economy that can point beyond toward a new society.
However, by their very nature, the attitudes and notions of moral economy exist at the level of appearances; rather than revealing the actual
relations, they reflect how things appear (and may necessarily appear) to
the real actors.

To illustrate this point, consider the spontaneous concepts of fairness characteristic of workers in capitalism—what we may call the moral
economy of workers within capitalism. In the mid-nineteenth century,
Marx observed that 99 percent of the wage struggles followed changes
that had led wages to fall. "In one word," he noted, they were "reactions
of labour against the previous action of capital."[37] In short, those wage
struggles were an attempt to restore the *traditional standard of life* which
was under attack.[38]

The spontaneous impulse of workers under these conditions was to
struggle for "fairness" against the violations of existing norms—indeed,
to fight a guerrilla war against effects initiated by capital. Their explicit
goal was to struggle for "a fair day's wage for a fair day's work." In doing
so, they were not attempting to change the system nor, indeed, struggling against exploitation (except insofar as exploitation was understood
as unfairness). Accordingly, Marx described the demands of workers as
"conservative" and argued that, instead of those demands for fairness,
"they ought to inscribe on their banner the *revolutionary* watchword,
'Abolition of the wages system!' "[39]

Yet Marx understood quite well why the workers' slogan focused
upon fair wages and a fair workday: it flows from the necessary appearance of a transaction in which the worker yields the property right to use
her capacity to work (that is, her labor power) for a given period. "On

the surface of bourgeois society," Marx pointed out, "the worker's wage appears as the price of labour, as a certain quantity of money that is paid for a certain quantity of labour."[40] Thus the conscious struggle of workers is over the fairness of "the certain quantity of money" and the fairness of the "certain quantity of labour." What is perceived as just and fair is that they receive an equivalent for their labor—that they are not "cheated." From the form of the wage as the payment for a given workday comes "all the notions of justice held by both the worker and the capitalist."[41]

"Nothing is easier," Marx commented, "to understand than the necessity, the *raison d'être*, of this form of appearance" that underlies the moral economy of the working class in capitalism.[42] On the surface, the worker sells her labor to the capitalist. However, this form of appearance "makes the actual relation invisible, and indeed presents to the eye the precise opposite of that relation."[43] Specifically, there appears to be no exploitation, no division of the workday into necessary and surplus labor; rather, all labor appears as paid labor. Precisely because exploitation is hidden on the surface, it is necessary to delve below the surface: "The forms of appearance are reproduced directly and spontaneously, as current and usual modes of thought; the essential relation must first be discovered by science."[44]

At the level of appearances, Marx argued, we cannot understand capitalism—"the interconnection of the reproduction process is not understood." After all, what in this case ensures the reproduction of the working class? As I argue in "The Fallacy of Everyday Notions":

> Only "when viewed as a connected whole," when we view capitalist and worker not as individuals but "in their totality, as the capitalist class and the working class confronting each other"—i.e., when we turn away from the way things necessarily appear to individual actors, can we understand the essential structural requirement for the existence of capitalism as a system—the necessity for the reproduction of wage-laborers.[45]

This is what Marx did in *Capital*. Considering workers as a whole, he assumed that in return for yielding to the capitalist the use of their capacities they receive their "traditional standard of life," what is necessary to reproduce themselves as wage laborers in a given time and place. This concept of a given level of necessity (the basis for the value of labor-power) allowed him to demonstrate how the workday was divided into necessary labor and surplus labor and how exploitation of workers was the necessary condition for the reproduction of capitalists.

For this critical deduction, Marx did not have to explain the source of this existing standard of necessity. Indeed, he simply assumed it as a given—an assumption he intended to remove in his projected book on wage labor.[46] With this approach, Marx was able to reveal the nature of capital and its inherent tendencies—something that a focus upon appearances (the sale of a specific quantity of labor by workers) could never reveal. Thus the case was made for the necessity to end capitalist relations of production rather than to struggle for "fair wages."

How else could we understand what capital is without the critique of those forms of appearance that underlie the moral economy of the working class in capitalism (and the political economy of capital)? Indeed, the apparent relation of exchange between capitalist and worker strengthens the rule of capital: it "mystifies" the actual relation and "ensures the perpetuation of the specific relationship of dependency, endowing it with the deceptive *illusion* of a transaction."[47] To enable workers to go beyond that conservative motto to the "*revolutionary* watchword," Marx offered the weapon of critique—a critique based upon an alternative political economy, the political economy of the working class.[48]

THE POLITICAL ECONOMY OF THE WORKING CLASS

What is the political economy of the working class? In *Beyond CAPITAL: Marx's Political Economy of the Working Class*, I recalled Marx's comments in the "Inaugural Address" of the First International about the victory of the political economy of the working class over the political economy of capital as the result of the restriction of the workday through the Ten Hours' Bill and the "still greater victory of the political economy of labour" with the development of cooperative factories. What, I asked, was this political economy which Marx introduced that encompassed both victories?[49]

One part of my answer focused upon the importance of the combination of workers and the struggle against those who separate them.[50] But this is only part of the political economy of the working class. To set out that political economy more fully than in *Beyond CAPITAL*, let us contrast it with the political economy of capital, the political economy that Marx critiqued in *Capital*.

First, whereas the political economy of capital focuses upon surface phenomena (prices, wages, rent, profits, and the way things appear to the individual actors), the political economy of the working class goes beneath the surface to examine the underlying structure and the necessary conditions for the reproduction of that structure. For example, it focuses upon the labor that underlies the output of particular use-values and sees in commodity prices (and their movements) the manner in which a commodity-money economy does what every economy must do—allocate society's labor to satisfy society's demands.

Second, we have seen that the political economy of capital accepts the appearance that the worker receives an equivalent for the given quantity of labor she provides to the capitalist. Accordingly, it concludes that the worker is not exploited and that profits are the result of the capitalist's own contribution. In contrast, Marx's political economy of the working class considers the relations of production under capitalism and demonstrates that the reproduction of those relations requires the exploitation of the worker.

Third, for the political economy of capital, the growth of output and productivity is the result of investment, that is, the accumulation of capital; and this occurs because the capitalist makes a sacrifice by not consuming all of the profits he has obtained as the result of his contribution. In contrast, for the political economy of the working class, the growth of output and productivity is in essence the product of the combination of workers—both the combination of current labor and the combination of current labor with the products of past social labor. From this perspective, the allocation of money (the representative of social labor) by the capitalist to investment is the form by which a capitalist society allocates labor to the means of production for expansion of future output.[51]

Finally, for the political economy of capital, the supreme goal is the growth of capital—that is, the accumulation of capital; and, to this end, anything that acts as a barrier to the growth of capital must be removed. In contrast, for the political economy of the working class, the supreme goal is the full development of human capacities; and, anything that acts as a barrier to full human development must be removed. Marx understood that "all means for the development of production" under capitalism "distort the worker into a fragment of a man," degrade him and "alienate him from the intellectual potentialities of the labour process."[52] Very simply, production under capitalist relations not only leads to exploitation (thereby producing capital) but also to the *deformation* of workers, thereby producing "poor human beings."[53] Thus, capitalism must be removed.

For the political economy of the working class, both exploitation and deformation of workers flow from capitalist relations of production. They are not separate and distinct—they interact. Consider the buying and selling of labor-power. What the capitalist purchases is the right to use the existing capacity of the worker as he wishes in a given time period. That, as Marx demonstrated, allows the capitalist to compel the worker to perform surplus labor and thereby produce the surplus value that, if realized, is the basis of capital. We see, then, that capital is the worker's own product and that our own product is turned against us.

When we consider this process explicitly from the side of the worker, though, we recognize that what workers yield to the capitalist for that given time period in this contract, however, is more than their existing capacity. They also surrender to the capitalist what is potentially "time for the full development of the individual, which in turn reacts back upon the productive power of labour as itself the greatest productive power."[54] Within the process of capitalist production, that time for development of her capacities is lost for the worker, and "it cannot be otherwise in a mode of production in which the worker exists to satisfy the need of the existing values for valorization."[55] Within these relations, rather than satisfying "the worker's own need for development," the worker's time is "devoted to the self-valorization of capital."[56]

Accordingly, that need for self-development necessarily appears as a need to *negate* labor-time. "Time for education, for intellectual development, for the fulfillment of social functions, for social intercourse, for the free play of the vital forces of his body and mind"—all these appear as the need for "*free* time" rather than as the need to transform the relations of production.[57] This focus upon reducing the workday quantitatively is clearly deficient, however, because it does not grasp the key link of human development and practice (the simultaneous changing of circumstances and self-change). Once we understand that every process of activity generates a human being who is formed by that activity as a joint product, it is obvious that labor under capitalist relations does not merely *divert* workers from the opportunity to satisfy their own need for development; it also *deforms* them, distorting "the worker into a fragment of a man."

Thus when the capitalist purchases the worker's capacity and utilizes it for his goal of expanding capital, he degrades not only her present but also her *future*. Production under capitalist relations, Marx proposed, has as its result "ignorance, brutalization and moral degradation."[58] *How could this not affect the worker as she enters into "free time"?* For the political economy of the working class, the reproduction of capitalism as a system is the reproduction of workers who will struggle for "fair wages" and a "fair workday," workers who look upon capitalist investment as in their interest, "a working class which by education, tradition and habit looks upon the requirements of this mode of production as self-evident natural laws."[59] In short, we understand that capitalism produces workers who tolerate their exploitation (because it is not apparent) but who are prepared to struggle against any violations of their concepts of fairness and justice—that is, violations of their moral economy.

But what determines the standards underlying those concepts—that is, the equilibrium that is the basis of consensus? This is not a question Marx explicitly considered theoretically. As indicated above, Marx began with the assumption that the traditional standard of life, the standard of necessity, was *given*. That assumption was sufficient for his immediate purpose to demonstrate that capital is the result of the exploitation of workers. *Beyond CAPITAL*, though, demonstrates that with the *removal* of this assumption of a fixed standard of life, it is no longer possible to argue that the automatic effect of productivity increases is the growth of exploitation (relative surplus value).[60] As Marx himself knew, as long as all other things are equal, the fall in the values of commodities with increasing productivity means that real wages rise.[61] The condition, then, for the reproduction of the traditional standard of life is that all other things cannot be equal. To go beyond the level of appearances in order to understand the standard of necessity (and any movements in it), the state of class struggle is essential to consider.

For this purpose, I introduced as a variable the concept of "the degree of separation among workers," which implies that insofar as capitalists can increase the degree of separation among workers (as occurs with the displacement of workers by machinery), they can capture the fruits of productivity gains; and insofar as workers are successful in uniting (as when they "organize planned cooperation between the employed and the unemployed"), they can increase real wages and reduce the length and intensity of the workday.[62]

Consider, then, how such an underlying concept necessarily appears. A given degree of separation among workers implies the reproduction of a given standard of necessity—an equilibrium in which any deviations produce feedback tendencies to restore the norms. Insofar as those deviations are temporary, it strengthens the belief in the permanency of those particular norms.[63] On the other hand, if capital is successful in increasing the degree of separation of workers (that is, if workers are unable to counteract capital's assault), then the tendency will be the development of a new, lower set of norms, a new equilibrium.

To understand the moral economy of the working class in capitalism, it is necessary to look for underlying factors that produce an apparent equilibrium. To attempt to go beneath the surface is essential. Similarly, to understand the moral economy of the working class in Real Socialism, we need to investigate its inner basis.

Beyond the Moral Economy of Real Socialism

The right of everyone to subsistence and growing living standards, the importance of stable prices and full employment, the orientation toward egalitarianism (and thus low income differentials)— all these were part of the norms that formed the moral economy of the working class in Real Socialism. This popular consensus of justice and fairness was regularly reproduced and thus strengthened as the result of feedback when deviations from an apparent equilibrium occurred.

Feedback and a tendency toward equilibrium is precisely what Kornai identified when he noted that "where developments in the real sphere generate results which deviate from existing norms (the result of 'habit, convention, tacit or legally supported social acceptance, or conformity'), the system generates signals that are fed back into the system via the control sphere."[64] Kornai argued that central decision makers in Hungary had as a target a normal rate of growth of real consumption per head of 3 to 4 percent with the result that "if the growth of consumption remains below its normal rate, the scale of investment will be reduced so as to leave more of the national income for consumption."[65]

It was very clear to Kornai why the vanguard acted in this way. Those at the top, he argued, were limited by what "the population is content to accept, and where dissatisfaction begins." There was a potential cost to violating the norms. "Holding back increases in living standards, or their absolute reduction, and infringing the lower limit . . . sooner or later entails serious political and social consequences, tension and even shocks, which after a shorter or longer lag force a correction."[66] In short, behind the attempt of the vanguard to avoid deviations from the norm was the anticipation of the responses of workers (for example, to increased prices). People, he recognized, wanted price stability, "and after a time they even expect the government to guarantee it. Any important price increase gives rise to unrest."[67] Accordingly, the question before the vanguard was—at what point would dissatisfaction start "to endanger the stability of the system"?

But why did workers react this way to perceived violations of existing norms? It wasn't because workers in Real Socialism felt that they were not getting a fair wage for a fair day's work. Behind the workers' view of fairness was not the appearance (as in the case of capitalism) that they were selling a certain quantity of labor in exchange for a certain quantity of money. In short, they were not moved by their failure to receive "in accordance with their contribution." Indeed, this was the very criticism made by the reformers—that the existing norms in Real Socialism were *not* based upon what they called "the socialist principle." As Gorbachev put it, there were "serious infractions of the socialist principle of distribution according to work."

On the contrary, the sense of entitlement of workers was based upon the concept of the common ownership of the means of production. Workers had this in common—they were all owners. The means of production were the property of the whole; and, since workers were part of the whole, this was the source of their entitlement. If they are common owners of means of production, though, the producers are in a relation of *equality*. They all must have access to the means of production and must have the opportunity to engage in labor and to secure the fruits of that ownership. Further, the tendency will be toward equal incomes—precisely because all are equal as owners of means of production.[68] Here, too, was the basis for latent outrage over evidence of individual wealth and privilege—to the extent workers knew about these (which is why it was characteristic of the vanguard to hide such "abuses" of common ownership).

These aspects of the moral economy of the working class did not drop from the sky. Rather, these concepts of fairness and justice were regularly reinforced by the statements of the vanguard itself. Workers were entitled because the state owned the means of production, and this was a workers' state. Naturally, it was understood that workers could not receive all of the current output. Since the moral economy involved the expectation that future consumption would be higher, a portion of their entitlement as owners necessarily was set aside for investment in the expansion of means of production. They understood, too, that this was a decision made by the vanguard (rather than one over which they had control). However, they could react to what was grasped as a political decision. This is why deviations from accepted norms tended to generate a political feedback from all those affected.

In short, the combination of worker responses to violations of fairness and vanguard anticipations of these generated what Thompson called "a particular equilibrium between paternalist authority and the crowd." That equilibrium in Real Socialism appeared as the result of an implicit agreement in which the workers yield the power to decide in return for the vanguard's guarantees. However, "nothing is easier to understand than the necessity, the *raison d'être*, of this form of appearance."[69] To reveal the underlying relations that produce these forms of appearance in Real Socialism, we must turn to the political economy of the working class.

Recall our discussion of vanguard relations and their reproduction in chapters 3 and 4. We saw that characteristic of these relations is that (except insofar as the managers have succeeded in making inroads) the vanguard exercises all the attributes of ownership of the means of production. While the vanguard assigns particular property rights (for example, job rights) to workers within the social contract, the entire bundle of property rights belongs to the vanguard as a collective owner.

And the productive relations reproduce those relations of distribution. Under the direction and command of the vanguard, the producers are subordinated to a plan drawn up by the vanguard, and their activity is subjected to its authority and purpose. Within this relation, workers are exploited (and would be even if they were to be the ultimate recipients of the fruits of their surplus labor). They furthermore are deformed within this relation. While the vanguard attempts to develop productive forces to achieve its preconceived goal, "all means for the development of production" under vanguard relations "distort the worker into a fragment of a man," degrade him and "alienate him from the intellectual potentialities of the labour process." This result must be entered as negative in any accounting system that values human development.[70]

Production under vanguard relations produces a working class consistent with the maintenance of vanguard relations. And, on its side, the vanguard retains its ability to command and to decide upon the allocation of the output. It determines what workers will receive as their current rations and how and where surpluses over and above this are invested. Within vanguard relations, both vanguard and workers are reproduced.

As long as the vanguard is able to satisfy what workers view as just and workers continue to accept this situation, the apparent reciprocity between vanguard and working class "mystifies" the actual relation and "ensures the perpetuation of the specific relationship of dependency, endowing it with the deceptive *illusion* of a transaction."[71] To go beyond mystification and the illusion of a transaction requires us to go beyond moral economy to the political economy of the working class.

As in the case of the underlying basis of the traditional standard of life of workers within capitalism, the degree of separation of workers is central in determining the terms of the social contract between vanguard and workers. Insofar as there is an apparent equilibrium, one that reinforces the sense of justice and fairness characteristic of the moral economy of the working class, it reflects a constant degree of separation among workers. Real Socialism in this case produces workers who tolerate their exploitation (because it is not apparent) but who are prepared to struggle against any violations of their concepts of fairness and justice—that is, violations of their moral economy.

That social contract, however, is not fixed in stone. If workers were able to reduce the atomism generated by vanguard relations and thereby increase their unity, they could rewrite the social contract in their favor. Conversely, for the vanguard to rewrite the social contract in its favor (or end it entirely), it must act against the existing institutions in order to increase the degree of separation of workers. One way by which the patterns associated with the moral economy of the working class can be assaulted by the vanguard is repression. With the advance of the logic of capital within Real Socialism, however, a more prevalent way (although not exclusive of repression) occurs when the vanguard initiates a move toward *khozraschet*—that is, economic accounting based upon economic and organizational separation of economic units.

In stressing that the income of workers should be linked to the profitability of individual enterprises, the vanguard attempts to dislodge the concept of the common ownership of the means of production upon which the moral economy of the working class rests. It moves to put an end to those "serious infractions of the socialist principle of distribution according to work." Indeed, the exhortations about "the socialist principle" are the clearest sign of the Battle of Ideas against the working class in Real Socialism.

Thus, in place of the equality of workers as common owners of the means of production, the push now is to separate workers into their own worlds. Rather than receiving an entitlement based upon being members of the whole, they become dependent upon the management of their individual enterprises—a profound increase in the degree of separation among workers. Further, to the extent that this focus upon individual enterprise accounting brings with it the removal of restrictions with respect to the release of workers, a division grows between the employed and the unemployed. *Khozraschet* represents not only the capture of property rights from the vanguard by incipient capitalists; it also brings with it the loss of job rights, the displacement of workers, the creation of a reserve army of the unemployed, and the attack on egalitarianism.

This development is not only the end to the apparent social contract, that is, of this particular mode of regulation; it also assembles all the elements of capitalist victory. In the absence of a workers' alternative (indeed, a socialist alternative) in the Battle of Ideas—one that identifies the source of exploitation and deformation in Real Socialism—this result is inevitable.

7—Toward a Society of Associated Conductors

In the society of associated conductors, producers cooperate in the process of producing for their needs and simultaneously produce themselves as socialist human beings. It is a society in which people are able to develop their full potential, that "rich individuality which is as all-sided in its production as in its consumption." In the society of associated conductors, producers are no longer means to someone else's end; rather there is what Marx called "the inverse situation, in which objective wealth is there to satisfy the worker's own need for development." [1]

Human development is at the core of this society—not through the delivery of gifts from above but through the activity of free and associated producers. As noted in the Introduction, this is a society characterized by democracy as protagonism: "Democracy in this sense—protagonistic democracy in the workplace, protagonism in neighborhoods, communities, communes—is the democracy of people who are transforming themselves into revolutionary subjects."

Real Socialism, a society divided into conductors and the conducted, was clearly not a society of associated conductors. That was its fundamental contradiction.

THE FUNDAMENTAL CONTRADICTION OF REAL SOCIALISM

The fundamental contradiction of Real Socialism is inherent in vanguard relations of production. Although the immediate source of crisis was the struggle between the logic of the vanguard and the logic of capital, the underlying basis was the nature of a society divided into conductor and the conducted, that is, between vanguard and the working class.

Characteristic of vanguard relations is that the domination over workers prevents the development of their capacities, ensures their alienation from the production process, and holds back the development of productivity, that is to say, the development of the productive forces of workers. However, this is only one side of those relations. The other side is the drive of the vanguard to push for growth, for the expanded reproduction of means of production, with the explicit purpose of building socialism.

Given the nature of the workers produced under vanguard relations, however, the vanguard must rely upon managers to act on its behalf to ensure the achievement of its goals. Yet the managers, who have a particular relation to the means of production (that is, possess those means of production), increasingly become conscious of their own particular interests; they act according to a logic of their own that is not identical to the logic of the vanguard. The managers indeed emerge as a class in itself; and their efforts to pursue their own interests interact with the attempts of the vanguard to enforce its property rights.

Thus the struggle between vanguard and managers displaces the relation between vanguard and workers as the contradiction producing the particular movement of Real Socialism. That contested reproduction generates a crisis that historically has led to the logic of the vanguard being increasingly subordinated by the logic of capital. This crisis cannot be resolved by "reforms." For one, no reform as such resolves the fundamental contradiction of Real Socialism—the domination of workers by the vanguard. For another, every new step in this process of subordination by emerging capital, every despotic inroad on the property rights of the vanguard, reveals yet another inadequacy in a system that still contains the logic of the vanguard. Accordingly, capital is compelled to make further inroads upon vanguard relations in order to produce all its own conditions of existence. And, it does—with the aid of the vanguard state.

Is there no alternative exit from Real Socialism—one that goes beyond vanguard relations in the direction of socialism?

The Germs of Socialism

Socialism does not drop from the sky "nor from the womb of the self-positing Idea" (which is to say, from the minds of theorists). Rather, it comes "from within and in antithesis" to the existing society.[2] This means we cannot ignore the specifics of those societies. In *Build It Now*, I argued: "Every society has its unique characteristics—its unique histories, traditions (including religious and indigenous ones), its mythologies, its heroes who have struggled for a better world, and the particular capacities that people have developed in the process of struggle."[3]

We need to understand the people within these societies—in particular, what they identify as fair and just. If we want to look beyond Real Socialism, can we ignore the moral economy of the working class that has been produced and reproduced within those societies? In E. P. Thompson's words, "If a future is to be made, it must be made in some part from these. It will not be made out of some Theorist's head."[4]

In itself, the moral economy of the working class does not point beyond Real Socialism. Rather, in the absence of changes in the underlying structure, the interaction between the moral economy of the working class and the concern of the vanguard about worker responses to deviations from existing norms tends to generate feedback mechanisms that restore an apparent equilibrium. But were there any latent elements present in the ideas of the working class from which a socialist future could be made?

In their orientation toward egalitarianism, we can see glimpses of one such characteristic—the focus upon the common ownership of the means of production. To the extent that workers in Real Socialism accept that they are common owners, they may feel they are entitled to share equally as owners (thereby implicitly asserting that the distribution of the fruits of production should correspond to the distribution of the owner-ship of the means of production). As the repeated exhortations of the vanguard against egalitarianism demonstrate, this sense of entitlement had lasting power in the minds of workers.

The social contract fostered and reinforced this aspect of the moral economy of the working class. However, that moral economy broke deci-sively with the perspective of the vanguard with respect to the popular consensus about theft by individuals. State property "was collective, i.e. partly their property after all!"[5] This was not the only way, however, in which the ideas of the working class departed from the ideas embodied in vanguard relations.

Workers also learned from their own experience within the sphere of production. The shortage economy, with the uncertainty produced by "the fluctuating quantity and quality of inputs on the one side, and the pressure from plan targets on the other," stimulated what Burawoy called "the workers' spontaneous collaboration." He argued that it was their collective improvisation and "spontaneous cooperation that made pro-duction possible in the socialist factory." The effect was to build solidarity within the workplace: "A shortage economy required a spontaneous and flexible specialisation on the shop floor that gave rise to solidarities that could fuel a working-class movement against state socialism."[6]

From the workplace thus came a particular common sense: the moral economy of workers contained a sense of their own collective power as workers and latent support for workers' control. However, unlike the "conception of distributive and social justice that gave central place to material welfare and egalitarianism," which, according to Cook, party and people shared, this was certainly not something "the Soviet state delivered."[7] On the contrary, inherent in vanguard relations was *oppos-ition* to worker power and decisions from below.

Of course, no organized campaign for worker power was possible in normal circumstances under the conditions imposed by the vanguard. Workers, though, did not wait for a violation of existing norms to engage in "resistance ranging from shirking, grumbling, foot dragging, false compliance, dissimulation, and other 'weapons of the weak.'"[8] There was a broad consensus among workers and support for resistance to domination and exploitation from above. Class struggle, as represented by individual acts and the support they received, was an essential part of a process of deepening the consensus among workers.

But what allows us to propose that the set of ideas of workers in Real Socialism included an orientation toward workers' power? Very simply, just as Thompson identified in the spontaneous food riots of the eighteenth century an underlying moral economy of the crowd, so does the spontaneous emergence of workers' councils at points of weakness in the system allow us to infer the existence of an underlying consensus among workers. What is the probability of observing developments such as those in Hungary in 1956 and Poland in 1980 in the absence of the presence of these elements in the moral economy of the working class in Real Socialism?[9]

There is an additional reason for assigning a high probability to the orientation toward worker decision making—the actions of the vanguard itself when it sought to shore up support for its role. In Yugoslavia in 1950 and Czechoslovakia in 1968, the vanguard demonstrated its own belief about what would move workers by introducing self-management of individual workplaces, and their understanding of the perspective of workers in Real Socialism was validated by the enthusiastic embrace of this option by workers.[10] Perestroika initially included gestures in this direction as well, but these were quickly undermined by the power of the managers and the retreat of the vanguard.[11]

Two elements are latent in the moral economy of the working class— social ownership of the means of production and social production organized by workers, that is, two sides of the socialist triangle described in this book's Introduction (and developed in *The Socialist Alternative*). Both imply the concept of "the cooperative society based on the common ownership of the means of production." Yet cooperation within a society involves more than cooperation within the sphere of production (even if production is understood to include activity outside formal workplaces, for example, within communities). It also encompasses cooperation with respect to the determination of the *purpose* of productive activity. Fully developed, such a society focuses directly upon social needs, that is, on production for communal needs and purposes—the third side of the socialist triangle. That side, too, is latent in the moral economy of the working class within "Real Socialism."

For that third side, the key concept is solidarity. In the solidarian society, people do not relate as owners, demanding a quid pro quo for parting with their property or their labor. Their starting point is not that of self-oriented owners, but rather the concept of a community: "a communal production, communality is presupposed as the basis of production." Our activity as members of the community is the "offspring of association." It is "posited from the outset as social labour," as labor for all, and the product of our activity "is a communal, general product from the outset."[12] In the solidarian society, we produce ourselves as conscious social beings: there is "*communal* activity and *communal* enjoyment— i.e., activity and enjoyment manifested and affirmed in *actual* direct *association* with other men."[13]

The germ of such relations is present in the relations among people within Real Socialism when they help one another without demanding an equivalent in return. For Ledeneva, *blat* was such a relation—one that "engenders regard for and trust in the other over the long term." In contrast to a relation in which alienated, mutually indifferent individuals exchange alienated things, she proposed that *blat* relations were similar to gift exchange insofar as the latter "underwrites social relations and is concerned with social reproduction." *Blat* builds upon social relations that already exist, and the reciprocity in those relations is "created and preserved by a mutual sense of 'fairness' and trust." In *blat* relations, people are available to each other, understand each other's values and there is "a set of normative obligations to provide assistance to others so they can carry out their projects."[14]

An "economy of favours" is how Ledeneva described the Soviet Union. And the concept of a "gift" that she introduces is significant because the solidarian society is precisely a "gift economy"—one in which those who give are rewarded not by the anticipation of what they may receive at some point in return but rather by the way in which they "construct themselves as certain kinds of people, and build and maintain certain relationships of debt and care."[15] Characteristic of the gift economy is that those who receive in this relation also give—not because reciprocity is externally imposed but because *not* to give violates one's own sense of virtue and honor. The gift relation thus presumes people who have a bond, people who have a past and hope to have a future, and its product is the enhancement of solidarity.

Acting within this relation builds trust and solidarity among people, and its joint product is people who are different from the products of exchange relations. Rather than your needs being the means "for giving me power over you" (as in the relation of exchange between "mutually indifferent persons"), by producing consciously to satisfy your needs, I look upon my activity as having worth. In Marx's words, "I would have directly *confirmed* and *realised* my true nature, my *human* nature, my *communal* nature."[16]

In gift relations, givers are rewarded "because thinking about another person's happiness" frees them: "Liberation results from relinquishing considerations of personal benefit to affirm a commitment to caring for another person."[17] In such a relation, one does what one can to the best of one's ability—as in the case of "mothering." Activity and enjoyment are one; our activity becomes "life's prime want." In the moral economy of the working class in Real Socialism, we can glimpse not only the orientation to social ownership of the means of production and social production organized by workers but also communal needs and purposes as the goal of productive activity—the third side of the socialist triangle.

Latent in the moral economy of the working class of Real Socialism is the potential for a different type of society—a cooperative society in which people relate consciously as members of a community. It is a society in which cooperation itself is a process of gift-giving, where we can develop all our powers without restraint. Rather than a society divided into conductors and conducted, this is a society of "free individuality based on the universal development of individuals and on the subordination of their communal, social productivity as their social wealth."[18]

In the society of associated conductors, "productive forces have also increased with the all-round development of the individual, and all the springs of co-operative wealth flow more abundantly."[19] Whereas the productive forces developed within capitalism and vanguard relations "distort the worker into a fragment of a man" and "alienate from him the intellectual potentialities of the labour process," in contrast the particular productive forces generated within socialist relations foster the all-round development of the producers.

No one could ever confuse this impulse with the logic of the vanguard; nor, obviously, is it the logic of capital. This is the logic of the working class, the logic of associated producers. It is a logic that places full human development at its core and insists that people develop through their activity—one which grasps the "key link . . . the coincidence of the changing of circumstances and of human activity or self-change."

For that society of associated producers to be developed, however, the elements of the old society must be subordinated. The necessary process is one of "subordinating all elements of society to itself, or in creating out of it the organs it still lacks. This is historically how it becomes a totality."[20]

Subordinating Vanguard Relations

What is necessary, then, for the development of socialism as an organic system? Let us review how capitalism emerged as an organic system. As discussed in *The Socialist Alternative*, the historical sequence involved in the "becoming" of capitalism proceeded from (a) *the emergence of a particular subordinated social relation* (that is, merchant and moneylending capital) that developed within precapitalist productive relations.[21] At a certain point, there was (b) *a rupture in property rights* with the result that those who were oriented to the expansion of capital became owners of the means of production (for example, land) and were in the position to determine the character of production and to introduce capitalist relations of production.

Yet, though the rupture of property rights was a necessary historical precondition, it was not a *sufficient* condition for capitalist relations of production: those peasants separated from the means of production could either rent land or sell their labor-power. In short, there was a further condition: it was necessary for capital to "seize possession of production" to establish the capital relation; only then, when workers were now compelled to sell their labor-power to survive, could we speak of (c) *the emergence of a new relation of production*.

The reproduction of this relation remained tenuous, however, so long as the "subordination of labour to capital was only formal"—that is, while capital was still dependent upon premises (in particular, the mode of production) inherited from the previous society. Accordingly, (d) *development of a specific mode of production* was the means by which capitalism produced its own premises spontaneously—that is, became a self-reproducing system that rests upon its own foundations. Yet until that time when capital was successful in developing a specifically capitalist mode of production, it required a specifically capitalist mode of regulation (the coercive power of the capitalist state) to ensure the reproduction of capitalist relations.[22]

In this context, let us speculate about a process of transcending Real Socialism. We have already suggested the route by which *capitalist* relations emerge and subordinate Real Socialism: the managers are successful in ending the power of the state to direct them and they thereby gain property rights over the means of production (the rupture), seize possession of production, and use the state to ensure the destruction of the power of both vanguard and workers. Our concern here, though, is with the possibility of an alternative *socialist* path from Real Socialism.

The social relation among workers within Real Socialism includes solidarity within individual workplaces and communities, a shared view of themselves as collective owners of the means of production and the general understanding that domination by the vanguard prevents all workers from acting collectively on their own behalf. It is the last of these that in a moment of crisis can lead workers to challenge the existing rule by the vanguard.

Given state ownership of the means of production, no juridical rupture in property rights would be necessary for workers. However, as we have seen, the real owner of the means of production in general and within individual units of production (to the extent that it controls the managers) is the vanguard. Accordingly, a rupture is required both in general and in particular to make the means of production the real property of the working class. "The replacement of possession by the state administration with ownership-exercise by society as a whole" (in Hegedus's words) as well as replacement of managerial power with the power of workers is the rupture that is necessary for the development of democratic control by the working class in both the state and individual units of production.

But what is democratic control? Within both workplace and society, the ability of workers to choose those who manage ruptures ownership by the vanguard party. Election of managers by workers in each workplace and election of the governing bodies of society would affect property rights over the means of production. *But this would not be sufficient to change the relations of production.* Even if those at the top are now responsible to those below, the real relations of conductor and conducted are unchanged. The result is that hierarchical relations can easily restore a class division within society: the managers can dominate the workers, and the state can stand over and above society—even though the faces of those who dominate may change.

New relations of production require the workers to seize possession of production. Where workers' councils emerge to direct activity, dispose of the means of production, and determine the use of surplus products (and, in the process, end the division between thinking and doing), a new relation of production would be established—one where workers are able to develop their capacities. Yet those new relations must not only be produced—they must be reproduced. And that is not at all an automatic process.

In the absence of a specifically socialist mode of production that "develops a working class which by education, tradition, and habit looks upon the requirements of that mode of production as self-evident natural laws," there is always the potential for the non-reproduction of socialist relations.[23] Until socialism develops as an organic system, its elements exist alongside elements of different systems. Under the concrete circumstances of "Real Socialism," a mode of regulation must be developed that subordinates the logic of both vanguard and capital. However, it also must subordinate the spontaneous tendencies characteristic of workers produced within "Real Socialism."

The Birthmarks of the Old Society

The society of associated producers necessarily emerges "in every respect, economically, morally and intellectually, still stamped with the birth marks of the old society." It cannot produce its own premises at the outset any more than capitalism could. It inevitably will be dependent upon elements that must be subordinated.

But what are those elements? To speak about birthmarks that affect the new society "economically, morally and intellectually" is to begin by talking about people formed with particular ideas within the old society. Accordingly, we need to ask again, *who are the people produced within Real Socialism?*

Not all characteristics of workers produced and reproduced within Real Socialism point in the direction of the society of associated producers. One that does not is their orientation toward self-interest. Consider the behavior of workers in the workplace under vanguard relations. In the sphere of production, we see people who are self-oriented and focused upon increasing income and reducing the length and intensity of the workday. They are alienated from their activity and from the products of their labor. Workers, after all, are active participants in the process of "storming," and they do so without regard to those inferior products created in the process. If they were not focused upon their bonuses but upon use-values, how could such waste continue to be produced? These are not people who think about the interests of society.

Further, their treatment of state-owned means of production reveals a tendency toward spontaneous privatization. For some, theft of materials is for the purpose of direct exchange with others who have money or other materials; for others, the theft is for the purpose of using the means of production as inputs for producing goods and services as part of the "second economy." Indeed, the very existence of that second economy (or "shadow economy") is significant. Although it did not only involve stolen state property, the size of that sector in the USSR at the end of the 1980s indicates the extent to which the state economy was not the only productive relation within which people functioned: more than a fifth of the working population (some 30 million people) was engaged in the shadow economy, and "in some branches of the service sector (house-building and repairs, car repairs), it was responsible for between 30 and 50 per cent of all the work undertaken."[24]

It is likely an exaggeration to propose that such second-economy activities were so fundamental to the day-to-day working of Soviet society that "the system could not have functioned" without them.[25] However, those activities clearly were intertwined with the social contract: "The low intensity and low productivity of the working day, which were at the heart of the 'social contract' between workers and the state, facilitated 'work on the side' (cultivation of private plots, etc)."[26] Naturally, those who expend time and energy in shadow-economy activity rationally want to minimize the intensity of their work in their formal state employment.

In defending a workday of low intensity as well as the actions of individuals, there is solidarity among these workers, but it is the solidarity of alienated workers; and it is solidarity within boundaries—those of the working group. Although there may be solidarity with other workers over common grievances (like price increases), the solidarity produced within the workplace is not an abstract solidarity focused upon society as a whole but is oriented to the specific group. Insofar as the goal of workers within this group is to maximize their income, they work together to ensure success in following the dictates of the plan and thereby securing the associated bonus rewards. It is not a great leap, then, to suggest that, if freed from the domination of instructions from above, they would be spontaneously inclined to work together to follow the dictates of the market as an *alternative* means of maximizing income.

Thus, rejecting their powerlessness in the workplace, the aspirations of workers in Real Socialism may lead them in the direction of a market self-management model characteristic of the former Yugoslavia. To realize such a latent goal, of course, would require workers to encroach upon the property rights of both the vanguard and the managers. By removing controls both *over* the enterprises (by the vanguard) and also *within* the enterprises (by managers), workers could transform the means of production they possess by virtue of their job rights into their own group property. They then would be in the position to manage the enterprises (which, as in Yugoslavia, could remain juridical state property) and to produce for the market with the goal of maximizing income per member of the enterprise.

We need to recognize, however, that there can be a significant difference between the form and essence of worker-management. Within Real Socialism, these workers are the product of a clear division between thinking and doing. In the absence of having developed the knowledge to self-manage, the desire to maximize income generates a spontaneous tendency to follow those who do have this knowledge—managers and experts. The wisdom of "we do our job well and we expect managers to do their job well" that emerged with market self-management in Yugoslavia can logically follow. Worker-management can become the rubber-stamping of proposals by experts rather than the development of the capacities of workers. In this case, the form of worker-management can be present but not its essence.

There is the possibility that workers can progressively develop the technical capacity to self-manage. But as long as the overriding goal is that of maximizing income per worker, developing their individual and collective capacities may be suspended in order to succeed in the market. This is only one element of a socialist society that is suspended when collective (but circumscribed) self-interest dominates. By putting workers into competition with one another, market self-management tends to produce a society marked by inequality and the absence of solidarity.[27] As such, it threatens *other* relations among workers in Real Socialism— their relations *outside* the workplace, outside of vanguard relations.

What the market yields, after all, differs for all working groups. As commodity-sellers within a market, the fortunes of each working group depend not only upon their own efforts but also upon luck and access to particular means of production. In the absence of a focus upon solidarity with other workers or society as a whole, the probability of significant inequality (as occurred in market self-management in Yugoslavia) is high. This is a disease that kills solidarity within society.[28]

But can lack of solidarity between workplaces within the society be counteracted by solidarity within the community? In other words, when we look at the concept of the gift economy as manifested in the relations among people within Real Socialism, can we see the potential for preventing growing inequality and the lack of development of human capacities? Again, we have to note some of the deficiencies inherent in the producers produced within Real Socialism. Those social relations that latently contain within them the concept of the gift economy exist, as we have seen, as relations within small networks. Here again, the solidarity is solidarity within boundaries—*group* solidarity.

Within these gift relations, the recipient of the gift always has a face. In other words, there are families, networks, and grouplets where the solidarity of the gift economy exists. Outside of these particular horizontal links, however, solidarity is only latent; within them, society in the abstract has little relevance. On occasion it is possible to mobilize people successfully from above to cooperate in the general interest of society in order to meet specific goals (harvests, irrigation works, etc.) or to deal with crises (floods and hurricanes, etc.). However, orientation to the abstract needs of society does not flow spontaneously from the networks of gift relations. It is faceless, with the result that such cooperation may appear as an externally imposed social duty rather than as a free expression of oneself.

For people formed within Real Socialism, participation in such activity may look like more of the same—alienated activity that requires attendance but does not stimulate activity in accordance with one's ability. The result of externally directed cooperation, indeed, may be "resistance ranging from shirking, grumbling, foot dragging, false compliance, dissimulation, and other 'weapons of the weak.'" The solidarian society that is the premise for productive activity for communal needs and purposes does not develop spontaneously.

If social production organized by workers and production for social needs are both infected as the new society emerges from the old, so also is the third side of the socialist triangle—social ownership of the means of production. What we see is the spontaneous tendency toward group property rather than social property. Insofar as the workers formed within Real Socialism possess their particular units of production and are oriented toward maximizing their income, their possession is turned into their property. As I wrote in *The Socialist Alternative*, "When differential possession or differential development of capacities (neither of which imply antagonism in themselves) are combined with self-interest and self-orientation to produce the belief in and desire for privileged entitlement, the tendency is toward the disintegration of the common ownership of the means of production."[29]

In short, though we can identify germs of a society of associated producers within Real Socialism, it is essential to recognize that these will appear initially in a flawed form. That is to be expected.[30] Further, those elements do not develop on their own in a vacuum. Rather, they exist alongside and interact with remnants of the logic of the vanguard and that of capital in a process of contested reproduction. This is the terrain for struggle. But how to struggle?

Questions Rather than Answers

Nothing is easier than to pull solutions out of one's back pocket. One need not explore particular, concrete circumstances if you already have the answers to all matters of interest. Whether it is the market and private property at one extreme or proletarian revolution and the correct application of Marxism-Leninism at the other—the mantra never ceases to comfort the intrepid. But it can be of little solace to those outside the particular fold.

When the disciple takes as his raw material "no longer reality" but inherited theory, "the *often paradoxical relationship of this theory to reality*" leads the disciple to "*explain away* reality." In this way, Marx commented in relation to Ricardo's disciples, "He demonstrates the beginning *disintegration of the theory* which he dogmatically espouses."[31]

We have attempted in this book to proceed from consideration of concrete phenomena and to develop theoretical insights that allow us to understand those phenomena.[32] But it does not mean we now have all the answers, that we can now declare, "Here is truth, kneel down before it!"[33] On the contrary, what our examination of Real Socialism generates are questions rather than answers—questions, in particular, as to the possibilities for building a society of associated producers from the old society of Real Socialism.

There are many reasons why we end up with questions. For one, all experiences of Real Socialism are not identical. Insofar as a new society necessarily emerges in a process of struggle of contested reproduction, the material conditions, the correlation of forces, and the particular capacities that people have developed may differ in each concrete case; as a result, when the matter (as all history) revolves around struggle, the answers may not be identical.

Thus, in contrast to my book *The Socialist Alternative: Real Human Development*, which explicitly set out a general path to socialism with concrete measures, specific organs of a new society, characteristics of a socialist mode of regulation, and a transitional program, our ambitions here are more modest. We ask, simply, what was and is possible within Real Socialism other than a march to capitalism? And we do so not with solutions that fall from the sky (or from our back pockets) or that come from "the womb of the self-positing Idea" but with questions inherent in the specifics of these particular societies we have been considering.[34]

Two questions in particular present themselves. Firstly, can workers in Real Socialism succeed in rupturing existing property rights, and can they proceed to "seize possession of production"—that is, can they establish new socialist relations of production? Secondly, can they succeed in ensuring the *reproduction* of those productive relations—that is, in the absence of a specifically socialist mode of production, can they develop a socialist mode of regulation that supports the reproduction of the new system before it becomes an organic system?

Let us begin by considering some issues with respect to the first of these questions. The rupture of existing property rights in this case, as noted above, involves a democratic revolution in both workplaces and state. Is this likely in the absence of a significant crisis—given the moral economy of the working class in Real Socialism? Is it likely—given that a characteristic of these workers is acceptance of the existing social contract (and the exploitation it supports)? Though occasional eruptions do occur when there is a violation of the social norms embodied in that contract, as long as the vanguard can restore the old equilibrium, the working class produced within Real Socialism tends not to challenge that pattern of decision making.

But what happens when there is a sustained crisis, when those who rule can no longer rule in the accustomed way by observing the social contract? As matters deteriorate, will workers accept the argument of the vanguard that the crisis has been due to errors such as violations of "the socialist principle" in the social contract and that the solution to the crisis is to unleash the development of the productive forces? Further, in the absence of an articulated logic of the working class, can the growing hegemony of the logic of capital (and the particular rupture of property rights this implies) be avoided?

Let's assume that the particular conditions within a country do permit a democratic change that transfers the power to make decisions to the working class. This development can occur much more easily within individual units of production than in society as a whole and may be fostered there by the vanguard itself (as a way to maintain vanguard relations in society at large). Whether this shift occurs at the level of individual units (through, for example, creation of workers' councils with juridical power) or at the level of the economy as a whole, this change in itself would not be sufficient to create new socialist relations of production. Unless the working class seizes possession of production and breaks down the division of thinking and doing through a process of protagonism at every level, doesn't someone else rule?

In individual units of production, it is possible for workers immediately to begin to exercise real ownership through workers' councils. And that is important in terms of the development of their capacities. At the level of society as a whole, however, for workers' goals and decisions to guide activity requires the development of an entire complex of organs— individual workers' councils, coordinating bodies of workers' councils, and organs that transmit the identification of needs (communal councils, communes, etc). Can these be established by fiat or does this involve a protracted process of learning and development? And if the latter, is it possible to avoid unevenness?

What happens if workers in self-managed enterprises focus upon their own collective self-interest by attempting to maximize income per worker? If they do so by relying upon managers and experts for all key decisions, doesn't this ensure that their own capacities remain underdeveloped and that the logic of capital is strengthened? Further, isn't the spontaneous tendency one of growing inequality—unequal access within society to particular means of production and unequal incomes, that is, unequal group property rather than social property?

In this situation, who speaks for the working class as a whole? Who has the responsibility for dealing with inequality and the existence of unemployment? At what point would less-privileged workers and those who find abhorrent the destruction of the equality and solidarity that does exist (that is, those aspects of the moral economy supported by the social contract) increasingly wish for a restoration of vanguard rela-tions—a return to what Thompson called "a particular set of relations, a particular equilibrium between paternalist authority and the crowd"?

In the absence of the articulation and enforcement of the logic of the working class—a logic that stresses the necessity for building solidarity immediately—is there an institution to which people produced within the old society can turn that is not a state over and above society as a whole? In the absence of the development of the organs of a state from below, how is it possible to avoid the emergence of a new conductor?

How stable, in short, are socialist relations of production as they emerge "in every respect, economically, morally and intellectually, still stamped with the birthmarks of the old society"? Under conditions of contested reproduction, where the logic of the vanguard and the logic of capital con-tinue to infect the new society, what is the mode of regulation that could permit the reproduction of new socialist relations of production?

And then, there is always the question of the actors. Given the nature of people produced within Real Socialism, who are the subjects who can bring about both the creation of socialist relations and their repro-duction? What forms of organization and coordination can succeed in subordinating not only the logic of the vanguard and the logic of capital but also the spontaneous tendencies and defects produced by the old society? And in this process, can members of the vanguard play a role—given the nature of their formation?

These are questions that need to be asked—not only to understand better the tragedies of the past but also to avoid the repetition of his-tory. There are no easy answers. However, one thing is certain—in the

ideological struggle, whatever our circumstances, we need to try to artic-
ulate what is implicit in current concepts and struggles and to develop
a conscious vision of a new society. At the core of such a vision, I have
argued, is the concept of the "key link" of human development and practice. To this end, I proposed in *The Socialist Alternative* a simple set of
propositions, a "Charter for Human Development" that can be recognized as self-evident requirements for human development:

1. Everyone has the right to share in the social heritage of human
    beings—an equal right to the use and benefits of the products of the
    social brain and the social hand—in order to be able to develop his
    or her full potential.
2. Everyone has the right to be able to develop their full potential and
    capacities through democracy, participation, and protagonism in
    the workplace and society—a process in which these subjects of
    activity have the precondition of the health and education that per-
    mit them to make full use of this opportunity.
3. Everyone has the right to live in a society in which human beings
    and nature can be nurtured—a society in which we can develop
    our full potential in communities based upon cooperation and
    solidarity.[35]

Another thing is certain: it is not possible to build a society of associated conductors in the absence of a theory that articulates the logic of the
working class.

8—Good-bye to Vanguard Marxism

After having considered the nature of vanguard relations of production, the contradictions within Real Socialism, the tendency for the emergence of capitalist relations and for an attack on the working class in Real Socialism, any further discussion may seem anti-climactic. However, it is important not to conclude without considering the theory that has accompanied and provided support for those developments. The problem of Real Socialism as such is not the result of the particular circumstances (for example, economic backwardness) under which a correct theory was applied. On the contrary, Vanguard Marxism is deformed Marxism, and if it is not challenged, the results of its application will be essentially the same under any conditions.[1]

Vanguard Marxism as One-Sided

"One-sided Marxism," I argued in *Beyond CAPITAL*, is seriously flawed because of its failure to focus upon the side of the worker.[2] Marx's *Capital* had an essential purpose—to arm workers by revealing the underlying nature of capital. The failure to understand, however, that *Capital* had a limited object, that it was a study not of capitalism as a whole but only of the side of capital, contributed to a distortion of Marx's thought and contribution.

Economic determinism and the functionalism that insists that whatever happens is the result of capital's needs was one aspect of this distortion. For one-sided Marxism, I argued, "if the workday declines, it is because capital needs workers to rest. If the real wage rises, it is because capital needs to resolve the problem of realization. If a public health care system is introduced, it is because capital needs healthy workers and needs to reduce its own costs." And on and on *ad nauseam*. The point was simple: when the needs and struggles of workers are ignored, "it cannot be considered surprising that a one-sided Marxism will find in the results of all real struggles a correspondence to capital's needs."[3]

This, however, was only one characteristic of one-sided Marxism. When you do not focus upon the side of workers, you don't even grasp the side of capital correctly. You don't recognize, for example, that insofar as workers are subjects, capital must find ways to divide and separate them in order to achieve its own goals. Thus, within capitalism as a whole, the impulse to defeat workers is present in everything that capital does. In short, when capital reorganizes the workplace or introduces new productive forces, its purpose is not efficiency as such but embodies the need to defeat workers in order to increase profits.

If we forget that new productive forces emerge within particular relations of production and are marked by class struggle characteristic of those relations, "the clear tendency is to think in terms of the autonomous development of productive forces and the neutrality of technology. Both conceptions are characteristic of economism."[4] In part, the problem emanated in Marx's inability to go beyond *Capital* to complete his own work; though far more serious was the failure of Marx's disciples to understand that capitalism is a totality marked by two-sided class struggle. This makes "the acceptance of economism as well as of deterministic and automatic objective laws easy."[5]

We need to go beyond *Capital* if we are to understand the side of workers. Limited to the themes of *Capital*, we do not grasp the importance of struggle as a process of producing and transforming people. And not only class struggle as such—*every* activity produces the people engaged in it. This is the core concept of Marx's focus upon practice—"the simultaneous changing of circumstances and human activity or self-change"; it is Marx's essential insight—what we have called "the key link" of human development and practice. Failing to stress this, we lose sight of Marx's consistent emphasis upon human development—upon the "rich human being," upon the development of a "rich individuality," upon the "development of all human powers as such the end in itself."[6]

Not to focus upon the forgotten "joint product" of capitalist production—the human beings that capitalism produces—is to minimize Marx's insistence upon how production within capitalist relations cripples workers. One-sided Marxism focuses upon exploitation rather than deformation, upon how much capital takes from the worker (which is, of course, capital's focus) rather than upon the empty, fragmented human beings who look upon capital's needs as "self-evident natural laws." Extracted surpluses, accumulation of capital, and the development of productive forces are its themes rather than the way capitalist relations of production thwart "the worker's own need for development."[7]

Since one-sided Marxism considers the worker primarily insofar as he or she exists for capital, insofar as he or she is exploited by capital, it naturally obscures the relevance of the other sides of that worker as a human being within society. Thus it ignores the relations other than wage labor in which people produce themselves (thereby stripping them of all determinateness other than as workers). Accordingly, it is blind to the way in which their struggles in those other relations (versus patriarchy, racism, national oppression, etc.) transform those people and how they enter into all their relations as these changed human beings.[8]

In this particular respect, one-sided Marxism is much like the political economy of capital that Marx condemned in 1844—political economy that looked at the proletarian only as a working animal to enrich capital, which did "not consider him, when he is not working, as a human being."[9] For Marx, such one-sidedness continued to be a matter of concern: see, for example, his explicit comment in 1875 about a view of producers who are considered "from one *definite* side only, for instance in the present case, are regarded *only as workers* and nothing more is seen in them, everything else being ignored."[10]

"Let us now rise above the level of political economy," Marx proposed.[11] Unfortunately, Vanguard Marxism does not rise above the level of the political economy of capital. Although it rejects the perspective of capital, it reproduces the one-sidedness of that political economy through its complete neglect of the existence of a particular joint product—the nature of workers produced under vanguard relations of production. Vanguard Marxism does not consider how workers are deformed by their lack of power to make decisions and to develop their capacities through their activity. How could it be denied that Vanguard Marxism is one-sided?

Further, since Vanguard Marxism does not view the worker as a subject (either within the formal production process or outside), it does not explore the behavior of workers subsumed within vanguard relations of production. Nor does it consider the other sides of those workers—for example, the other relations within which workers exist, such as their communities, their networks of friends and family, and their common position as members of a society with common ownership of the means of production. In regarding them "*only as workers*... everything else being ignored," Vanguard Marxism offers a caricature of workers in Real Socialism.

This one-sidedness permeates Vanguard Marxism. It is reflected in, among other aspects, the disappearance of relations of production, the focus upon the march of neutral productive forces and the passage from a stage of socialism to that of communism. But Vanguard Marxism is more than one-sided. It is also a rejection of a dialectical perspective.

VANGUARD MARXISM AS A REJECTION OF A DIALECTICAL WORLDVIEW

Characteristic of a dialectical worldview is the focus upon the whole and the interaction of parts within the whole. As we have seen in the discussion of the "system paradigm" in chapter 1 and the political economy of the working class in chapter 6, Marx stressed the concept of a totality whose elements "all form the members of a totality, distinctions within a unity" and where "mutual interaction takes place between the different moments."[12] In this focus upon the whole, we are describing what Lukács viewed as the basis of a scientific revolution: "The category of totality, the all-pervasive supremacy of the whole over the parts is the essence of the method which Marx took over from Hegel and brilliantly transformed into the foundations of a wholly new science."[13]

Characteristic of such a view is the recognition of what Lenin described in his notes on Hegel's *Science of Logic* as "the universal, all-sided, *vital* connection of everything with everything":

> A river and the *drops* in this river. The position of *every* drop, its relation to the others; its connection with the others; the direction of its movement; its speed; the line of the movement—straight, curved, circular, etc. upwards, downwards. The sum of the movement. . . . There you have a *peu près* [approximately] the picture of the world according to Hegel's *Logic*—of course minus God and the Absolute.[14]

From this perspective, one cannot look at individual parts as isolated (with their own intrinsic properties), independent and indifferent to each other; rather, we understand the parts as "members of a totality," where there is "reciprocal action of these various sides on one another."[15] And, in that interaction, those parts interpenetrate; they "re-create each other by interacting and are re-created by the wholes of which they are parts."[16] Accordingly, a view of change as the result of exogenous stimuli is difficult to sustain. As Lenin noted in his reading of Hegel, "The all-sidedness and all-embracing character of the interconnection of the world . . . is only one-sidedly, fragmentarily and incompletely expressed by causality."[17]

To understand society as a totality is to understand that its change and development is not a simple relationship of cause and effect, of independent and dependent variables. A dialectical worldview necessarily rejects a perspective that ignores the interaction of parts within the whole or that offers a concept of change based upon a single cause. It follows that it necessarily rejects Vanguard Marxism.

Consider, for example, how the relations of production disappear because of the one-sidedness of Vanguard Marxism. Since the nature of the workers produced under vanguard relations is not a subject of inquiry, there is no requirement to investigate those relations. Vanguard Marxism, though, identifies the relations of production with juridical ownership of the means of production; thus it does not *need* to introduce a separate variable for the former. The story Vanguard Marxism tells is that building the new society depends upon the development of productive forces, its only real variable.

Why, according to Vanguard Marxism, do the productive forces develop? Very simply, they develop because the vanguard ensures their development. Thus, from the single cause of developing productive forces, we are led to the ultimate mover—the conductor. Of course, the conductor is not all-powerful; he cannot develop the new society fully at the outset. He must lead this society from a lower stage, socialism, to a higher stage, communism, a movement from the realm of necessity to a society marked by abundance. The story Vanguard Marxism tells is simple. With the ending of capitalist ownership of the means of production, the conductor can deliver the passengers to the promised land of abundance (where we can be like "the lilies of the field who toil not, neither do they spin").[18]

This simple linear account of progress has little in common with a dialectical view of society as a totality. As Marx scoffed about Proudhon's theory, "How, indeed, could the single logical formula of movement, of sequence, of time, explain the structure of society, in which all relations coexist simultaneously and support one another?"[19]

Without considering the nature of the people produced within vanguard relations of production, Vanguard Marxism cannot explore how the productive forces are marked by the character of vanguard relations, including class struggle within those relations. Nor is it able to think about the worker as she interacts with other workers in the workplace, in her relations with others in society outside the workplace or as a member of a society in which common ownership of the means of production is presumed. The way in which these elements act upon (and are acted upon by) other elements in this structure of society is a closed book for Vanguard Marxism.

Nevertheless, the story that Vanguard Marxism tells implicitly involves a particular view of the worker. And that is revealed by what it calls the "socialist principle." Before the conductor brings us to the end of the line (the realm of freedom), the question arises as to how "the quantity of products to be received by each" will be regulated at the first station where we stop (that is, the stage of socialism). For Vanguard Marxism, the answer is clear: "until the 'higher' phase of Communism arrives," there must be "the *strictest* control by society *and by the state* of the measure of labour and the measure of consumption."[20]

Thus a state is necessary, one which, "while safeguarding the public ownership of the means of production, would safeguard equality in labour and equality in the distribution of products."[21] To ensure this equality during this realm of necessity, the governing principle must be "the socialist principle," which links the quantity of products to be received by each to the quantity of labor performed by each. "An equal amount of products for an equal amount of labour," distribution in accordance with contribution.

Because Vanguard Marxism makes the implicit assumption that the worker in the stage of socialism is alienated from her labor and alienated from the products of her labor, it views this principle of distribution as necessary. This alienated worker must be regulated since she wants to minimize her labor and to maximize her consumption; in particular, the "socialist principle" of "to each according to his contribution" must be strictly enforced. By ensuring that those workers who contribute more will receive more, the vanguard concludes that workers will have an incentive to contribute more.

What in this view will happen if the "socialist principle" is ignored? Given that alienated workers look upon work as a burden, they will act as if they can satisfy their needs without having to work for items of consumption. So if productivity is low or fails to rise, Vanguard Marxism has a ready answer—"violations" of the socialist principle. The worker cannot be trusted to produce for the needs of society in the absence of a directing authority. To "safeguard equality in labour and equality in the distribution of products," state regulation is necessary. [22]

But, we are told, this situation is not permanent. It would be necessary only until there was an "enormous development of productive forces" that makes possible the ending of the antithesis between mental and physical labor. "The economic basis for the complete withering away of the state is such a high stage of Communism that the antithesis between mental and manual labour disappears." In this realm of abundance, society can now adopt the rule, "from each according to his ability, to each according to his needs," and the state can wither away.[23]

The promise is that there will come a time when the labor of people "becomes so productive that they will voluntarily work *according to their ability*." At this point, there would be "no need for society to regulate the quantity of products to be received by each; each will take freely 'according to his needs.'"[24] *But not yet.* The worker remains alienated from his labor and the products of his labor until such time as abundance permits his activity and enjoyment to be one—that is, for labor to be "life's prime want."[25]

There is nothing especially Marxist (or socialist) about this promise. Indeed, the idea that individual material self-interest (embodied in the "socialist principle") can and will guide us to the realm of freedom was expressed best by Keynes, a non-socialist and critic of Marxism:

> I see us free, therefore, to return to some of the most sure and certain principles of religion and traditional virtue—that avarice is a vice, that the exaction of usury is a misdemeanor, and the love of money is detestable, that those walk most truly in the paths of virtue and sane wisdom who take least thought for the morrow. We shall once more value ends above means and prefer the good to the useful. We shall honor those who can teach us how to pluck the hour and the day virtuously and well, the delightful people who are capable of taking direct enjoyment in things, the lilies of the field who toil not, neither do they spin.
>
> But beware! The time for all this is not yet. For at least another hundred years we must pretend to ourselves and to everyone that fair is foul and foul is fair; for foul is useful and fair is not. Avarice and usury and precaution must be our gods for a little longer still. For only they can lead us out of the tunnel of economic necessity into daylight.[26]

How different is Keynes's argument about the need to rely upon self-interest to lead us to abundance from the argument of Vanguard

Marxists? As part of their exhortation to put off everything until the appropriate productive forces have been developed, Vanguard Marxists invoke a statement by Marx in his *Critique of the Gotha Program*: "Right can never be higher than the economic structure of society and the cultural development conditioned thereby."[27] Their interpretation of this, however, is a complete distortion of Marx, not surprising given their reduction of the "economic structure of society" to the development of productive forces.

Consider again Marx's stress upon a "structure of society, in which all relations coexist simultaneously and support one another." This was a conception of a system in which the elements all interact. But those elements are not necessarily perfectly compatible, except in a "completed" organic system: "In the completed bourgeois system every economic relation presupposes every other in its bourgeois economic form, and everything posited is thus also a presupposition; this is the case with every organic system."[28]

Before the system produces its own premises and presuppositions, it must rely upon "historic" premises, those it inherits from the old society. The course of development of the new society necessarily involves the subordination of those elements it has inherited and the production of its own presuppositions—that is, when the latter emerge *"not as conditions of its arising but as results of its presence."*[29] As noted in chapter 1, Marx was clear about how a new organic system emerges: "Its development to its totality consists precisely in subordinating all elements of society to itself, or in creating out of it the organs which it still lacks. This is historically how it becomes a totality."[30]

This, we see in *Capital*, is the way capitalism emerged as "fully developed." Inevitably, the system is initially inadequate, but the point is to subordinate its inherited defects so that it can stand upon its own foundations. This distinction between the "becoming" and "being" of an organic system reappears in Marx's *Critique of the Gotha Program*, where he identified an "inevitable" defect in the new society "when it has just emerged after prolonged birth pangs from capitalist society." We begin with a society not "as it has *developed* on its own foundations, but, on the contrary, just as it *emerges* from capitalist society; which is thus in every respect, economically, morally and intellectually, still stamped with the birthmarks of the old society from whose womb it emerges."[31]

What exactly is that inevitable defect? It is that, despite replacing capitalist ownership with the common ownership of the means of production, within the new society there was the continuation of "bourgeois right"; in particular, labor power remains private property:

> The capitalist mode of production . . . rests on the fact that the material conditions of production are in the hands of non-workers in the form of property in capital and land, while the masses are only owners of the personal condition of production, of labour power.[32]

Continuation of this ownership has definite implications. As owners of labor-power, the producers act in their own self interest; like any owner, they demand the most for their property. The worker insists that he not be cheated, that "the same amount of labour which he has given to society in one form he receives back in another." Underlying this exchange of equivalents ("where a given amount of labour in one form is exchanged for an equal amount of labour in another form") is the private ownership of "the personal condition of production, of labour power." This is nothing more than the continuation of bourgeois right.[33]

This exchange relation, inherited by the new society "just as it *emerges* from capitalist society," is precisely what must be subordinated. The new society can only develop by "subordinating all elements of society to itself, or in creating out of it the organs which it still lacks." For the development of "rich human beings," of that "rich individuality which is as all-sided in its production as in its consumption," the *Critique of the Gotha Program* sees the necessity to end "the antithesis between mental and physical labour" and to ensure the "all-round development of the individual." It was inevitable at the outset that owners of labor-power would deem themselves entitled to an equivalent for their labor. However, Marx rejected this view of producers "only as workers" as one-sided, and he counterposed to the producer "as a private individual" the producer "in his capacity as a member of society."[34]

Unfortunately, Vanguard Marxism drew a different lesson from the *Critique of the Gotha Program* and applied it to a society that Marx never anticipated—one in which workers are dominated, deformed, and exploited under the direction of a vanguard. For Marx, the new society was to be a cooperative society based upon common ownership of the means of production, a society for which the cooperative factories of the nineteenth century were "the first examples of the emergence of a new form." The great merit of those cooperatives, he argued, had been to demonstrate practically that the domination of workers "can be superseded by the republican and beneficent system of the *association of free and equal producers*."[35] And, by abolishing the old division of labor that separated thinking and doing, those associated producers would create the conditions for "all-round development of the individual."[36]

But, as we have seen, the lesson that Vanguard Marxism extracted was the necessity to enforce the "socialist principle" in the lower stage of socialism. Rather than subordinate the inherited "defect," it insists upon *strengthening* it, that is, building upon the defect to build the new society.[37] For Vanguard Marxism, that defect would only be removed through the development of productive forces. So the *real* defect was the inadequate development of productive forces.

You won't find in Vanguard Marxism a focus upon the reciprocal action of the various sides of a whole or a concept of "the all-sidedness and all-embracing character of the interconnection of the world." Its linear conception, in which all history is the history of the development of productive forces, however, is not merely a rejection of a dialectical conception of a structure of society in which all elements interact; it is also a class perspective.

Vanguard Marxism as a Class Perspective

What makes a set of ideas a class perspective? Here, we can recall Marx's comments (quoted in chapter 5) about the ideological representatives of the petit bourgeoisie: "In their minds they do not get beyond the limits which the latter do not get beyond in life, that they are consequently driven, theoretically, to the same problems and solutions to which material interest and social position drive the latter practically."[38]

Consider the following thought experiment. Picture a society in which there is no exploitation, one where collective workers receive directly or indirectly all the fruits of their labor either immediately or ultimately within their lifetimes. If, in such a society, workers are directed from above, are prevented from developing their capacities (in particular, separated from the development of their intellectual capacities), remain alienated, and are focused upon the possession of things, could we consider this the society of the associated producers?

This is not to suggest that there was no exploitation of workers in Real Socialism. Rather, the thought experiment is useful because it demonstrates clearly that a society divided into conductors and the conducted (*even if there were no exploitation as such*) has little to do with anything to which Marx looked forward. Only a theoretical perspective that ignores the nature of people produced in every human activity, the human product that results from the simultaneous changing of circumstance and self-change, could fail to stress the deformation of people under vanguard relations of production.

That theoretical position is the same as the practical position of the vanguard. Just as the vanguard is oriented to maximize investment to achieve the highest possible growth of productive forces, just as the vanguard stresses the necessity of the state to direct from above, to expand production without regard for productive relations, and to determine the relation between output and consumption, so also does Vanguard Marxism provide the theoretical justification for the vanguard. Vanguard Marxism is the theoretical perspective of a conductor who believes that the working class must be led to the Promised Land and "that his business is to serve music and to interpret it faithfully." It is the theoretical perspective of those who stand above the working class. But also against the working class.

In addition to supporting vanguard relations that exploit and deform workers, Vanguard Marxism provides the theoretical justification for attacks on the moral economy of the working class in Real Socialism. Worker management, egalitarianism, and a focus on producing for the needs of others—all these seeds of a socialist society are declared to be premature.

In its view that these elements in the moral economy of the working class within Real Socialism should be postponed until the higher stage of communism, we can see how the one-sidedness that looks at producers "from one *definite* side only . . . *only as workers* and nothing more . . ." supports an attack on the existing working class. Anything contrary to the "socialist principle" is judged by Vanguard Marxism to be a violation that will be a fetter upon the development of productive forces and thus socialism. It is declared to be "alien to the proletariat."[39]

Vanguard Marxism and the political economy of the working class point in opposite directions. Whereas Vanguard Marxism stresses its "socialist principle" of distribution and attributes problems to the violations of that principle, the political economy of the working class says with Marx that it is "a mistake to make a fuss about so-called *distribution* and put the principal stress on it."[40] Marx insisted that relations of distribution correspond to specific relations of production, and that it is the latter upon which we must focus. This, then, is the context in which to understand his comment that "right can never be higher than the economic structure of society and its cultural development conditioned thereby."[41] For the political economy of the working class, the point is clear. "The economic structure of society" is its relations of production; change those and you change the culture of society. Change the relations of production and end alienation, exploitation, and deformation—that is, produce workers differently.

The problem is that the idea of changing the relations of production makes little sense to those who equate the relations of production with juridical ownership of the means of production and for whom the real relations of production are invisible. Since Vanguard Marxists view the alienation of producers as an inherited, historical presupposition rather than as a situation produced and reproduced every day within vanguard relations of production, they "do not get beyond the limits" theoretically that the vanguard does not get beyond in real life.

If we are serious about building a viable alternative to capitalism, we need to recognize the impact of the class perspective of Vanguard

Marxism. Insofar as it has identified socialism with juridical ownership and ignored the exploitation and deformation of workers under vanguard relations, it has tended to discredit both socialism and the Marxism in whose name all this occurs. Not only does this disarm workers within Real Socialism but it also sends a message to workers elsewhere that Marxism is consistent with the exploitation and deformation of workers.

Beyond Vanguard Marxism

Nothing in the above discussion (or anywhere in this book) should be interpreted as a critique of the necessity for leadership in the struggle against capital or to build a new socialist society. Nor should there be any doubt that building a society that allows for full human development must begin by ending capitalist ownership of the means of production by all means possible. Similarly, I do not question the necessity for a period to draw upon the inherited state (with all the dangers this poses) as part of a socialist mode of regulation.

This book, however, does not explore such questions. It has a limited object; it concentrates upon a particular phenomenon, Real Socialism, which consolidated in the period roughly following 1950. We need to learn from that experience if we are to build a society that allows for the full human development that Marx grasped as the right goal, a society of rich human beings. To do that, it is essential that we recognize the link between Vanguard Marxism and vanguard relations of production. Within Real Socialism, like the state coercion that prevents the independent organization of workers, Vanguard Marxism serves as a weapon in the hands of the vanguard against the working class. Outside Real Socialism, Vanguard Marxism offers a road map to Real Socialism and, beyond that, to the reemergence of capitalism.

How can we go beyond Vanguard Marxism? We do that by restoring Marxism as a philosophy of praxis and freedom. We do that by returning to a Marxism where human beings are the hub and where the focus is upon "the worker's own need for development." This means an emphasis upon the conditions in which people produce themselves through their own activity, upon the character of the relations of production and all of the social relations in which they act.

But that also means taking seriously the moral economy of the working class. As I indicated in chapter 6, "If workers struggle over the ideas and norms associated with moral economy, then clearly those ideas are a material force. By considering those social norms and beliefs as to what is right and what is wrong, we can root our analysis in the concrete." Through that analysis, "we also may be able to point to elements in the moral economy that can point beyond toward a new society." The ideas and concepts of right and fairness on the part of the working class need to be analyzed in order to understand what underlies those ideas—for the purpose of providing the working class with the weapons necessary to go beyond appearances.

We need a Marxism that articulates the logic of the working class, the logic of associated producers—one that points to the centrality of cooperation, the development of solidarity, protagonism, and the building of a society of "free individuality based on the universal development of individuals and on the subordination of their communal, social productivity as their social wealth."[42]

If that Marxism appropriately focuses upon the nature of people produced within particular relations of production, then the premise that abundance is a necessary precondition for such a society marked by community, solidarity, and equality appears questionable. The realm of freedom does not have to wait until the realm of necessity has been ended. On the contrary, "the true realm of freedom, the development of human powers as an end in itself," can be built *within* the realm of necessity itself and can redefine necessity.[43] Through the development of institutions that foster the development of human capacities, we can be brought to the point where our activity and enjoyment are one, where the exercise of our capacity, our labor, is our real need.

If we want to end the alienation among people that fosters their self-interest and a consumerism that both reproduces the separation of people and always leaves them wanting more, it is necessary to develop new institutions that permit people to transform themselves while transforming circumstances. In *The Socialist Alternative*, I identified such institutions and measures as the development of worker management, the strengthening of communal councils, the expansion of the commons, and the development of direct links between these cells of a new socialist state. Those specific ideas are not our concern here. What is essential, however, is that Marxists must break with the Vanguard Marxism that insists upon a conductor who stands over and above the conducted. For Marxists and all of those who want to build a socialist society, there is no place for a theory that does not put human development and practice at its center.

Vanguard Marxism comes in different varieties. There are those in power for whom it serves as theoretical justification of their position. There are also those far from power who accept the theory but whose main criticism of Real Socialism has been that it was the *wrong* vanguard in power. The latter group may be critical of the lack of workplace democracy and the evils of an ill-defined "bureaucracy," but as long as they embrace the theory of a conductor without whom the music of the future will never be realized they do not offer a real alternative. As long as their politics do not make the "key link" central to both theory and practice, that is, as long as they do not understand the importance of the simultaneous changing of circumstances and human activity or self-change, it is all more of the same.[44]

In practice, it is essential to build those institutions through which people are able to develop their capacities and make themselves fit to create a new world. But there is a theoretical condition as well. A philosophy of praxis, a philosophy of freedom, a political economy that expresses the logic of the working class—these are the characteristics of a Marxism that can be a weapon for the associated conductors. It is time to say good-bye to Vanguard Marxism.

Bibliography

Åhlander, Ann-Mari Sätre. *Environmental Problems in the Shortage Economy: The Legacy of Soviet Environmental Policy.* Cheltenham: Edward Elgar, 1994.

Allen, Robert C. *Farm to Factory: A Reinterpretation of the Soviet Industrial Revolution.* Princeton: Princeton University Press, 2003.

Bauer, Tamas. "Investment Cycles in Planned Economies." *Acta Oeconomica* (1978).

Berliner, Joseph S. *Proceedings. American Economic Review* (May 1966).

___. The Innovation Decision in Soviet Industry. Cambridge, MA: MIT Press, 1976.

___. *The Economics of the Good Society: The Variety of Economic Arrangements.* Oxford: Blackwell, 1999.

Bernik, Ivan. "Political Culture in Post-Socialist Transition: Radical Cultural Change or Adaptation on the Basis of Old Cultural Patterns?" *Frankfurt Institute for Transformation Studies* no. 09 (2000).

Bettelheim, Charles. *Economic Calculation and Forms of Property: An Essay on the Transition between Capitalism and Socialism.* New York: Monthly Review Press, 1975.

Bihari, Peter. "Hungary: Towards a Socialist Market Economy?" *Studies in Political Economy* 18 (Autumn 1985).

Brecht, Bertolt. "Songs for Children, Ulm 1592." In Bertolt Brecht, *Selected Poems,* trans. H. R. Hays. New York: Grove Press, 1959.

Brus, Wlodzimierz, and Kazimierz Laski. *From Marx to the Market: Socialism in Search of an Economic System.* Oxford: Clarendon Press, 1992.

Burawoy, Michael. "Working in the Tracks of State Socialism." *Capital & Class* 98 (Summer 2009).

Canetti, Elias. *Crowds and Power.* Middlesex: Penguin, 1973.

Cook, Linda J. *The Soviet Social Contract and Why It Failed: Welfare Policy and Workers' Politics from Brezhnev to Yeltsin.* Cambridge, MA: Harvard University Press, 1993.

David, Paul A. "Clio and the Economics of QWERTY." *American Economic Review* (May 1985).

Dobb, Maurice. *Socialist Planning: Some Problems.* London: Lawrence & Wishart, Ltd, 1970.

Ellman, Michael. "Economic Calculation in Socialist Economies." In *The New Palgrave: Problems of the Planned Economy,* ed. John Eatwell, Murray Milgate, and Peter Newman. New York: W. W. Norton, 1990.

___. *Socialist Planning.* Cambridge: Cambridge University Press, 1979.

Filzer, Donald A., ed. *The Crisis of Soviet Industrialization: Selected Essays of E. A. Preobrazhensky.* Armonk, NY: M. E. Sharpe, 1979.

Filzer, Donald A. *Soviet Workers and the Collapse of Perestroika: The Soviet Labour Process and Gorbachev's Reforms, 1985–1991.* Cambridge: Cambridge University Press, 1994.

Flaherty, Patrick. "Cycles and Crises in Statist Economies." *Review of Radical Political Economics* 24/2–3 (1992).

___. "Perestroika and the Neoliberal Project." In *The Socialist Register 1991,* ed. Ralph Miliband and Leo Panitch. London: Merlin, 1991.

___. "Perestroika and the Soviet Working Class." *Studies in Political Economy* 29 (Summer 1989).

___. "Recasting the Soviet State: Organizational Politics in the Gorbachev Era." *Socialist Register* (1988).

Goldman, Marshall I. "The Convergence of Environmental Disruption." In *Comparative Economic Systems: Models and Cases,* ed. Morris Bornstein. Homewood, IL: Richard D. Irwin, 1974.

Granick, David. "Central Physical Planning: Incentives and Job Rights." In *Comparative Economic Systems: An Assessment of Knowledge, Theory and Method,* ed. Andrew Zimbalist. Boston: Kluwer/Nijhoff, 1983.

___. *Enterprise Guidance in Eastern Europe: A Comparison of Four Socialist Economies.* Princeton: Princeton University Press, 1975.

___. *Job Rights in the Soviet Union: Their Consequences.* Cambridge: Cambridge University Press, 1987.

Hegedus, Andras. *Socialism and Bureaucracy.* London: Allison & Busby, 1976.

Hegel, G. W. F. *The Phenomenology of Mind.* New York: Harper Torchbooks, 1967.

Hewitt, Ed. "The Hungarian Economy: Lessons of the 1970s and Prospects for the 1980s." Paper presented to the Joint Economic Committee, U.S. Congress, February 1981.

High, Holly. "Cooperation as Gift versus Cooperation as Corvee." Paper presented at "Regenerations: New Leaders, New Visions in Southeast Asia," Council of Southeast Asian Studies, Yale University. Available at: http://www.freeebay.net/site/content/view/801/34/.

Jun, Li. "Collective Action of Laid-off Workers and Its Implication on Political Stability: Evidences from Northeast China." PhD diss., City University of Hong Kong, 2008.

Kagarlitsky, Boris. "Interview." *Against the Current*, March 3, 1995.

___. *The Dialectic of Change.* London: Verso, 1990.

Kantorovich, L. V. "Mathematical Formulation of the Problem of Optimal Planning." In Nove and Nuti, *Socialist Economics.*

Kernohan, Andrew. "Democratic Socialism and Private Property." *Studies in Political Economy*, Vol. 22, 1987.

Keynes, J. M. "Economic Possibilities for Our Grandchildren." In *Essays in Persuasion*, New York: W. W. Norton, 1963.

Kopstein, Jeffrey. "Workers' Resistance and the Demise of East Germany." Available at: http://libcom.org/history/workers-resistance-demise-east-germany-jeffrey-kopstein.

Kornai, János. *The Socialist System: The Political Economy of Communism.* Princeton: Princeton University Press, 1992.

___. *Anti-Equilibrium: On Economic Systems Theory and the Tasks of Research.* Amsterdam: North-Holland, 1971.

___. *Economics of Shortage.* Amsterdam, 1980.

___. *Growth, Shortage and Efficiency: A Macrodynamic Model of the Socialist Economy.* Berkeley: University of California Press, 1982.

___. *Overcentralization in Economic Administration: A Critical Analysis Based on Experience in Hungarian Light Industry.* Oxford: Oxford University Press, 1959.

___. *The Socialist System: The Political Economy of Communism.* Princeton: Princeton University Press, 1992.

___. "The System Paradigm." Discussion Paper Series 58. Budapest: Collegium Budapest, Institute for Advanced Study, July 1999.

Kosolapov, Richard. *Problems of Socialist Theory.* Moscow: Progress Publishers, 1974.

___. *Socialism: Questions of Theory.* Moscow: Progress Publishers, 1979.

Kosygin, A. N. "On Improving Industrial Management." In Nove and Nuti, *Socialist Economics.*

Kovanda, Karol. "Czechoslovak Workers' Councils." *Telos* 28 (Summer 1976).

Labor Focus on Eastern Europe, 5/1 & 2 (Spring 1982).

Laibman, David. "The 'State Capitalist' and 'Bureaucratic-Exploitative' Interpretations of the Soviet Social Formation: A Critique." *Review of Radical Political Economics* 10/4 (Winter 1978).

Lavigne, Marie. *The Socialist Economies of the Soviet Union and Europe,* White Plains, NY: International Arts and Science Press, 1974.

Lebowitz, Michael A. "Building on Defects: Theses on the Misinterpretation of Marx's Gotha Critique." *Science and Society* (October 2007).

___. "Holloway's Scream: Full of Sound and Fury." *Historical Materialism* 13/4 (2005).

___. "Kornai and Socialist Laws of Motion." *Studies in Political Economy* 18 (Autumn 1985).

___. "New Wings for Socialism." *Monthly Review* (April 2007).

___. "The Capitalist Workday, the Socialist Workday." *MRZine* (April 2008).

___. "The Socialist Fetter: A Cautionary Tale." In *The Socialist Register 1991,* ed. Ralph Miliband and Leo Panitch. London: Merlin, 1991.

___. "Trapped Inside a Box? Five Questions for Ben Fine." *Historical Materialism* 18/1 (2010).

___.*Beyond CAPITAL: Marx's Political Economy of the Working Class.* New York: Palgrave Macmillan, 2003.

___. *Build It Now: Socialism for the Twenty-first Century.* New York: Monthly Review Press, 2006.

___. *Following Marx: Method, Critique, and Crisis.* Chicago: Haymarket Books, 2009.

___. *The Socialist Alternative: Real Human Development.* New York: Monthly Review Press, 2010.

Ledeneva, Alena V. *Russia's Economy of Favours:* Blat, *Networking and Informal Exchange.* Cambridge: Cambridge University Press, 1998.

Lenin, V. I. *Philosophical Notebooks.* In Lenin, *Collected Works*, vol. 38. Moscow: Foreign Languages Publishing House, 1961.

___. *State and Revolution.* Peking: Foreign Languages Press, 1965.

Levins, Richard, and Richard Lewontin. *The Dialectical Biologist.* Cambridge: Harvard University Press, 1985.

Lewin, Moshe. *Political Undercurrents in Soviet Economic Debates: From Bukharin to the Modern Reformers.* London: Pluto Press, 1975.

___. *The Soviet Century.* London: Verso, 2005.

Liuhto, Kari T. "The Transformation of the Soviet Enterprise and Its Management: A Literature Review." University of Cambridge Working Paper no. 146, ESRC Centre for Business Research, September 1999.

Lomax, Bill. "The Working Class in the Hungarian Revolution." *Critique* (Autumn–Winter 1979–80).

Lukács, Georg. *History and Class Consciousness: Studies in Marxist Dialectics.* Cambridge, MA: MIT Press, 1972.

Mandel, David. "Economic Reform and Democracy in the Soviet Union." In *Socialist Register 1988.* ed. Ralph Miliband and Leo Panitch. London: Merlin, 1988.

___. *Perestroika and the Soviet People: Rebirth of the Labour Movement.* Montreal: Black Rose Books, 1991.

Manevich, Efim. *Labour in the USSR: Problems and Solutions.* Moscow: Progress Publishers, 1985.

Marx, Karl, and Frederick Engels. *The German Ideology.* In Marx and Engels, *Collected Works*, vol. 5. New York: International Publishers, 1976.

Marx, Karl. "Instructions to the Delegates of the Provisional General Council: The Different Questions." In *Minutes of the General Council of the First Interna-*

tional, 1864–66. Moscow: Foreign Languages Publishing House, n.d.

___. "The Eighteenth Brumaire of Louis Bonaparte." In Marx and Engels, *Selected Works.* Moscow: Foreign Languages Publishing House, 1951.

___. "Theses on Feuerbach." In Marx and Engels, *Collected Works,* vol. 6. New York: International Publishers, 1976.

___. "Value, Price and Profit." In *Collected Works of Marx and Engels,* vol. 20.

___. *Capital,* vol. 1. New York: Vintage Books, 1977.

___. *Capital,* vol. 3. New York: Vintage Books, 1981.

___. *Critique of the Gotha Programme.* In Marx and Engels, *Selected Works,* vol. 2. Moscow: Foreign Languages Publishing House, 1962.

___. *Economic Manuscript of 1861–63.* In Marx and Engels, *Collected Works.* vol. 30. New York: International Publishers, 1988.

___. *Grundrisse.* New York: Vintage Books, 1973.

___. *The Poverty of Philosophy.* In Marx and Engels, *Collected Works,* vol. 6. New York: International Publishers, 1976.

___. *Theories of Surplus Value,* vol. 3. Moscow: Progress Publishers, 1971.

Mészáros, István. *Beyond Capital: Toward a Theory of Transition.* New York: Monthly Review Press, 1995.

Montias, J. M. "Planning with Material Balances in Soviet-Type Economies." In Nove and Nuti, *Socialist Economics.*

New Times 9 (March 10, 1986).

Nove, Alec. "Economic Reforms in the USSR and Hungary, a Study in Contrasts." In Nove and Nuti, *Socialist Economics.*

___. *The Economics of Feasible Socialism Revisited.* London: HarperCollins Academic, 1991.

___. *The Soviet Economic System.* London: George Allen & Unwin, 1977.

Nove, Alec, and D. M. Nuti, eds. *Socialist Economics: Selected Readings.* Middlesex: Penguin Educational, 1974.

Osteen, Mark. "Jazzing the Gift: Improvisation, Reciprocity, Excess." *Rethinking Marxism* 22/4 (October 2010).

Pravda, Alex. "Industrial Workers and Political Development in the Soviet Union and Eastern Europe." National Council for Soviet and East European Research, 1981. Available at: http://www.ucis.pitt.edu/nceeer/1981-624-16-Pravda.pdf.

Preobrazhensky, Evgeny. *The New Economics.* Oxford: Clarendon Press, 1965.

Scanlan, James P. "From Samazidat to Perestroika: The Soviet Marxist Critique of Soviet Society." In *The Road to Disillusion: From Critical Marxism to Post-Communism in Eastern Europe,* ed. Ray Taras. Armonk, NY: M. E. Sharpe, 1991

Scott, James C. *The Moral Economy of the Peasant: Rebellion and Subsistence in Southeast Asia.* New Haven: Yale University Press, 1976.

Sik, Ota. *Czechoslovakia: The Bureaucratic Economy.* White Plains, NY: International Arts and Sciences Press, 1972.

Statutes of the Communist Party of Cuba. Havana: Political Publishing House,

1981.

Tablada, Carlos. *Che Guevara: Economics and Politics in the Transition to Socialism*. Sydney, Australia: Pathfinder, 1989.

Thompson, E. P. "The Moral Economy of the English Crowd in the Eighteenth Century." *Past and Present* 50 (1971).

Thompson, E. P. *The Poverty of Theory*. New York: Monthly Review Press, 1978.

Ticktin, Hillel. *Origins of the Crisis in the USSR: Essays on the Political Economy of a Disintegrating System*. Armonk, NY: M. E. Sharpe, 1992.

Workers' Liberty 10 (May 1988), excerpted from Kowalewski, Zbigniew. *Rendez-nous nos usines*. Paris: PEC, 1985.

Notes

Introduction: New Wings for Socialism

1. Bertolt Brecht, "Songs for Children, Ulm 1592," in *Selected Poems*, trans. H. R. Hays (New York: Grove Press, 1959).
2. The discussion in this first section draws directly upon "New Wings for Socialism," *Monthly Review* (April 2007) and a talk in January 2007 in Caracas on the occasion of the presentation of the Venezuelan edition of *Build It Now: Socialism for the 21ˢᵗ Century* (Monthly Review Press, 2006).
3. Michael A. Lebowitz, "The Socialist Fetter: A Cautionary Tale," *The Socialist Register 1991*, ed. Ralph Miliband and Leo Panitch (London: Merlin, 1991).
4. See my discussion of John Holloway's arguments in Michael A. Lebowitz, "Holloway's Scream: Full of Sound and Fury," *Historical Materialism* 13/4 (2005).
5. Marxist economists, in particular, tend to engage in spirited competition over who has correctly predicted the crisis—and do so with all the accuracy of a stopped watch.
6. On this question, see in particular Michael A. Lebowitz, *Beyond CAPITAL: Marx's Political Economy of the Working Class* (New York: Palgrave Macmillan, 2003).
7. Karl Marx, *Capital*, vol. 1 (New York: Vintage Books, 1977), 935.
8. Ibid., 1:548, 643, 799.
9. Ibid., 1:482–84, 548, 607–8, 614.
10. Karl Marx, *Grundrisse* (New York: Vintage Books, 1973), 488.
11. Ibid., 287; Lebowitz, *Beyond CAPITAL*, 32–44.
12. Marx, *Capital*, 1:899.

13. Ibid.
14. Lebowitz, *Beyond CAPITAL*, 177.
15. Marx, *Capital*, 1:772. This theme of human development is the focus in Michael A. Lebowitz, *The Socialist Alternative: Real Human Development* (New York: Monthly Review Press, 2010).
16. Lebowitz, *The Socialist Alternative*, chap. 1.
17. Karl Marx, "Theses on Feuerbach," in Marx and Engels, *Collected Works* (New York: International Publishers, 1976), 6:4.
18. Lebowitz, *The Socialist Alternative*, 50–55, 154–59.
19. See *Alo Presidente* # 263 and #264, http://www.alopresidente.gob.ve/.
20. The initial discussion of these three elements occurred in a paper written for Chávez in December 2006 at a time when I directed a program on Transformative Practice and Human Development at Centro Internacional Miranda in Venezuela. I drew upon this paper in January 2007 at the launch of the Venezuelan edition of *Build It Now*, referred to in n. 2.
21. Marx, *Grundrisse*, 278.

Overture: The Conductor and the Conducted

1.   Lebowitz, *Beyond CAPITAL*, 84–87.
2.   Marx, *Capital*, 1:448.
3.   Ibid., 1 449–50.
4.   Karl Marx, *Capital*, vol. 3 (New York: Vintage Books, 1981), 507–8.
5.   Ibid., 1:450.
6.   Ibid., 3:507.
7.   Ibid., 3:510–11.
8.   Ibid., 1:449.
9.   Elias Canetti, *Crowds and Power* (Middlesex: Penguin, 1973), 460.
10. Ibid., 459.
11. Lebowitz, *The Socialist Alternative*, 154–59.
12. Marx, *Capital*, 1:450; Lebowitz, *The Socialist Alternative*, 156.
13. Lebowitz, *The Socialist Alternative*, 86.
14. Marx, *Capital*, 1:447.
15. Ibid., 1:482.
16. Marx, *Grundrisse*, 87.
17. The manager in a cooperative factory paid by the workers (rather than representing capital to the workers) is another example he offered—one in which "the antithetical character of the supervisory work disappears." Cooperative factories, indeed, provided the proof that the capitalist was "superfluous as a functionary in production." Marx, *Capital*, 3:512, 510.
18. Canetti, *Crowds and Power*, 458.
19. This particular metaphor, too, can be the source of much disagreement among those who love classical music.

1. The Shortage Economy

1. Richard Kosolapov, *Socialism: Questions of Theory* (Moscow: Progress Publishers, 1979), 8, 11–2, 482.

2. See, for example, the discussions of Czechoslovakia and China in Richard Kosolapov, *Problems of Socialist Theory* (Moscow: Progress Publishers, 1974).

3. This division and ordering, which corresponds to Marx's distinction between the accumulation of capital within capitalism and the original accumulation of capital (that is, the "being" and "becoming" of capital, respectively) is not arbitrary. Marx was contemptuous of bourgeois economists who distorted the distinct nature of capital by "formulating the conditions of its becoming as the conditions of its contemporary realization" (Marx, *Grundrisse*, 460). Consideration of the consolidated system first is essential not only for understanding that system but also to guide historical inquiry. See the extended discussion in chapter 4, "The Being and Becoming of an Economic System," in Lebowitz, *The Socialist Alternative*.

4. Janos Kornai, *The System Paradigm*, Discussion Paper Series No. 58 (Budapest: Collegium Budapest, Institute for Advanced Study, July 1999), 4, 8.

5. Karl Marx, *The Poverty of Philosophy*, in Marx and Engels, *Collected Works*, vol. 6 (New York: International Publishers, 1976), 167; Marx, *Grundrisse*, 99.

6. Lukács argued: "The category of totality, the all-pervasive supremacy of the whole over the parts is the essence of the method which Marx took over from Hegel and brilliantly transformed into the foundations of a wholly new science." Georg Lukács, *History and Class Consciousness: Studies in Marxist Dialectics* (Cambridge, MA: MIT Press, 1972), 27.

7. Richard Levins and Richard Lewontin, *The Dialectical Biologist* (Cambridge, MA: Harvard University Press, 1985), 269, 273, 3; Lebowitz, *Beyond CAPITAL*, 52–54. As an illustration of his focus upon the whole, Kornai rejected the neoclassical premise of given individual preferences as a starting point and commented, "According to the system paradigm, individual preferences are largely the products of the system itself. If the system changes, so do the preferences." Kornai, *The System Paradigm*, 10.

8. Kornai, *The System Paradigm*, 9–10.

9. Marx, *Capital*, 1:711.

10. Ibid., 1:724. Marx demonstrated the continuity of his thought on the reproduction of capitalist relations of production by footnoting here his 1849 work, *Wage Labour and Capital*: "Capital presupposes wage-labour; wage-labour presupposes capital. They reciprocally condition each other's existence; they reciprocally bring forth each other. Does the worker in the cotton factory merely produce cotton goods? No, he produces capital." This idea of a "connected whole" characterized by two sides that bring forth each other can be found, too, in Marx's 1844 Manuscripts and subsequently

when he talked in *The Holy Family* (1845) about how "proletariat and wealth are opposites; as such they form a single whole." Lebowitz, *Beyond CAPITAL*, 205–6.

11. Marx, *Capital*, 3:957.

12. Marx, *Grundrisse*, 278.

13. Ibid.; Lebowitz, *The Socialist Alternative*, chap. 4.

14. Marx, *Capital*, 1:899.

15. Marx, *Grundrisse*, 694, 699.

16. Marx, *Capital*, 1:382, 899, 937. Similarly, to ensure reproduction of capitalist productive relations when workers are able to save in order to escape wage labor (as occurred, for example, in the North American settlements, where "today's wage-labourer is tomorrow's independent peasant or artisan, working for himself"), Marx argued that capital needed to use the state to introduce extraordinary, "artificial means." Ibid., 1:936–37, 911, 900; Lebowitz, *The Socialist Alternative*, 96–97.

17. Lebowitz, *The Socialist Alternative*, 94–99.

18. Marx, *Capital*, 1:931; Lebowitz, *The Socialist Alternative*, 97.

19. For a concrete discussion of a socialist mode of regulation, see chaps. 6 and 7 in Lebowitz, *The Socialist Alternative*.

20. Marx, *Capital*, 1:90; Marx, *Grundrisse*, 100–101; Lebowitz, *Beyond CAPITAL*, 54–55.

21. Marx, *Capital*, 1:102.

22. Marx, *Grundrisse*, 107. See the discussion of Marx's method in Michael A. Lebowitz, *Following Marx: Method, Critique, and Crisis* (Chicago: Haymarket Books, 2009), esp. part 2, "The Logic of Capital," and chap. 10, "Marx's Methodological Project as a Whole."

23. Marx, *Grundrisse*, 278; Janos Kornai, *The Socialist System: The Political Economy of Communism* (Princeton: Princeton University Press, 1992), 16.

24. Kornai, *The Socialist System*, 366.

25. Marx, *The Poverty of Philosophy*, 167.

26. Kornai, *The Socialist System*, 198, 500, 570, 366; Marx, *Grundrisse*, 278.

27. Kornai, *The Socialist System*, 368–69.

28. Ibid., 16.

29. The discussion here draws upon Michael A Lebowitz, "Kornai and Socialist Laws of Motion," *Studies in Political Economy* 18 (Autumn 1985).

30. Janos Kornai, *Economics of Shortage*, 2 vols. (Amsterdam, 1980), 457.

31. Alena V. Ledeneva, *Russia's Economy of Favours: Blat, Networking and Informal Exchange* (Cambridge: Cambridge University Press, 1998), 87.

32. Janos Kornai, *Economics of Shortage*, 29.

33. Michael Ellman, *Socialist Planning* (Cambridge: Cambridge University Press, 1979), 207.

34. Janos Kornai, *Anti–Equilibrium: On Economic Systems Theory and the Tasks of Research* (Amsterdam: North-Holland, 1971), 321.

35. Janos Kornai, *Overcentralization in Economic Administration: A Critical Analysis Based on Experience in Hungarian Light Industry* (Oxford: Oxford University Press, 1959), 168, 186.

36. Ibid., 215.

37. Kornai, *Economics of Shortage*, 547.

38. Ibid., 62–63.

39. Ibid., 63.

40. Ibid., 556.

41. Ibid., 191.

42. Ibid., 192–94.

43. Ibid., 402.

44. Ibid., 403.

45. Joseph Berliner, quoted in *Proceedings, American Economic Review* (May 1966): 157–58.

46. Joseph Berliner, *The Innovation Decision in Soviet Industry* (Cambridge, MA: MIT Press, 1976), 478, 481.

47. See the examples cited in Maurice Dobb, *Socialist Planning: Some Problems* (London: Lawrence & Wishart, 1970); Marie Lavigne, *The Socialist Economies of the Soviet Union and Europe* (White Plains, NY: International Arts and Science Press, 1974); and Alec Nove, *The Soviet Economic System* (London: George Allen & Unwin, 1977).

48. Kornai , *Overcentralization in Economic Administration*, 37.

49. Ibid., 132–33.

50. Boris Kagarlitsky, *The Dialectic of Change* (London: Verso, 1990), 248–49.

51. Dobb, *Socialist Planning: Some Problems*, 37n.

52. Kornai , *Overcentralization in Economic Administration*, 130.

53. Ibid., 141.

54. Ibid., 133.

55. Ota Šik, *Czechoslovakia: The Bureaucratic Economy* (White Plains, NY: International Arts and Sciences Press, 1972), 101–2.

56. Alec Nove, *The Economics of Feasible Socialism Revisited* (London: HarperCollins Academic, 1991), 22.

57. Šik, *Czechoslovakia: The Bureaucratic Economy*, 102.

58. Dobb, *Socialist Planning: Some Problems*, 38.

59. Kornai, *Overcentralization in Economic Administration*, 136.

60. Ibid., 137.

61. Ibid., 107.

62. Ibid., 178, 186.

63. Ibid., 186.

64. Ibid., 192.

65. Kornai, *Economics of Shortage*, 28.

66. Ibid., 110.

67. Ibid., 209–10, 306–11.

68.   Ibid., 566, 568.

2. The Social Contract

1.   See, for example, the discussion of principal-agent relations (or the "agency problem") in Joseph Berliner, *The Economics of the Good Society: the Variety of Economic Arrangements* (Oxford: Blackwell, 1999), 329–31, 339–43.

2.   Kornai, *The Socialist System*, 371. Kornai's rejection of a principal-agent model may be dismissed since he precluded it in any form *by definition* when he announced that "the motivations of the firm's management and of other groups in the bureaucracy will not be treated separately. The object is to identify the general inducements applying to all leaders in the economic bureaucracy" (118–19).

3.   Tamas Bauer, "Investment Cycles in Planned Economies," *Acta Oeconomica*, 21 (3) (1978).

4.   Patrick Flaherty, "Cycles and Crises in Statist Economies," *Review of Radical Political Economics* 24/3–4 (1992): 113.

5.   Ibid., 114.

6.   Ibid., 116.

7.   Ibid., 117.

8.   Ibid., 118.

9.   Ibid., 119

10.   Šik, *Czechoslovakia: The Bureaucratic Economy*, 46–50, 52.

11.   Moshe Lewin, *The Soviet Century* (London: Verso, 2005), 329–33, 370–71.

12.   Flaherty, "Cycles and Crises in Statist Economies," 117, 124.

13.   Kornai, *Economics of Shortage*, 380.

14.   Janos Kornai, *Growth, Shortage and Efficiency: A Macrodynamic Model of the Socialist Economy* (Berkeley: Univerity of California Press, 1982).

15.   Ibid.,   4–5, 24–33, 76; Kornai, *Economics of Shortage,* chap. 21; Lebowitz, "Kornai and Socialist Laws of Motion."

16.   Kornai, *Economics of Shortage*, 382.

17.   Kornai, *Growth, Shortage and Efficiency,* 47–48.

18.   Kornai, *Economics of Shortage*, 383.

19.   Ibid., 212.

20.   Ibid., 415.

21.   Ibid., 502–3.

22.   Ibid., 485.

23.   Ibid., 509–10.

24.   Ibid., 235.

25.   Ibid., 251–52.

26.   David Granick, *Enterprise Guidance in Eastern Europe: A Comparison of Four Socialist Economies* (Princeton: Princeton University Press, 1975), 245–46.

27.   Ibid., 473.

28. Kornai, *Economics of Shortage*, 254.

29. Ibid., 255.

30. Ibid., 256.

31. Granick, *Enterprise Guidance in Eastern Europe*, 249n.

32. David Granick, *Job Rights in the Soviet Union: Their Consequences* (Cambridge: Cambridge University Press, 1987), 69.

33. David Laibman, "The 'State Capitalist' and 'Bureaucratic-Exploitative' Interpretations of the Soviet Social Formation: A Critique," *Review of Radical Political Economics* 10/4 (Winter 1978): 29.

34. Granick, *Job Rights in the Soviet Union*, 103.

35. Lewin, *The Soviet Century*, 331.

36. Laibman, "The 'State Capitalist' and 'Bureaucratic-Exploitative' Interpretations of the Soviet Social Formation," 29.

37. Lewin, *The Soviet Century*, 176.

38. Granick, *Job Rights in the Soviet Union*, 13–14.

39. Ibid., 1–3.

40. David Granick, "Central Physical Planning: Incentives and Job Rights," in *Comparative Economic Systems: An Assessment of Knowledge, Theory and Method*, ed. Andrew Zimbalist (Boston: Kluwer/Nijhoff, 1983), 139.

41. Granick, *Enterprise Guidance in Eastern Europe*, 246.

42. Ed Hewitt, "The Hungarian Economy: Lessons of the 1970s and Prospects for the 1980s," paper presented to the Joint Economic Committee of the U.S. Congress, February 1981.

43. Linda J. Cook, *The Soviet Social Contract and Why It Failed: Welfare Policy and Workers' Politics from Brezhnev to Yeltsin* (Cambridge, MA: Harvard University Press, 1993), 1.

44. Laibman, "The 'State Capitalist' and 'Bureaucratic-Exploitative' Interpretations of the Soviet Social Formation," 28–9.

45. Laibman, "The 'State Capitalist' and 'Bureaucratic-Exploitative' Interpretations of the Soviet Social Formation," 28.

46. Donald A. Filzer, *Soviet Workers and the Collapse of Perestroika: The Soviet Labour Process and Gorbachev's Reforms, 1985–1991* (Cambridge: Cambridge University Press, 1994), 5.

47. Lewin, *The Soviet Century*, 320.

48. Cook, *The Soviet Social Contract and Why It Failed*.

49. Ibid., 3.

50. Patrick Flaherty, "Perestroika and the Soviet Working Class," *Studies in Political Economy* 29 (Summer 1989): 47. Flaherty cites a case of a young worker committed to a psychiatric hospital over her complaints concerning "enforcement of health and safety regulations in the shop and [her] vocal criticism of the maintenance of plush private dining quarters for management while workers went without" (46).

51. Boris Kagarlitsky, "Interview," *Against the Current*, March 3, 1995.

3. *The Nature and Reproduction of Vanguard Relations of Production*

1. Kornai, *The Socialist System*, 4, 11.
2. Ibid., 87.
3. Ibid., 375.
4. Ibid., 368.
5. Ibid., 375.
6. Ibid., 361.
7. Marx, *Capital*, 3:507.
8. Kornai, *The Socialist System*, 56.
9. Canetti, *Crowds and Power*, 458.
10. Kornai, *The Socialist System*, 55.
11. Note the discussion in Lebowitz, *The Socialist Alternative* (48–50), of the theories of Paulo Freire and their relation to Marx's rejection of the utopian concept of changing circumstances for people rather than revolutionary practice, in which people transform themselves in the process of transforming circumstances.
12. Kornai, *The Socialist System*, 41.
13. Ibid., 118–19.
14. See, for example, the first four duties of members of the Communist Party of Cuba in *Statutes of the Communist Party of Cuba* (Havana: Political Publishing House, 1981), 8.
15. See http://english.people.com.cn/data/organs/cpc.html.
16. Kornai, *The Socialist System*, 36.
17. Ibid., 57.
18. Ibid., 121.
19. Wlodzimierz Brus and Kazimierz Laski, *From Marx to the Market: Socialism in Search of an Economic System* (Oxford: Clarendon Press, 1992), 47.
20. Marx, *Capital*, 3:735–36.
21. Ibid., 1:739–41.
22. The conditions under which a second soul expands at the expense of the logic of the vanguard are explored later.
23. Kornai, *The Economics of Shortage*, 383, 212.
24. Kornai, *The Socialist System*, 45.
25. Ibid., 87, 50–51.
26. Ibid., 89.
27. Ibid., 93.
28. Ibid., 37, 39.
29. Ibid., 362.
30. Ibid., 33, 409.
31. Ibid., 161–62. Kornai notes that the orientation of the vanguard for "forced growth, rush and importunate haste" (and the tendency not to undertake investments "expressly to protect the environment"), plus the characteristic in Real Socialism "that there is no way of organizing in society independent,

strong environmental movements capable of confronting the economic decision makers if necessary" have obvious implications for the destruction of the environment (178). For descriptions of the extent of environmental damage in Real Socialism, see Marshall I. Goldman, "The Convergence of Environmental Disruption," in *Comparative Economic Systems: Models and Cases,* ed. Morris Bornstein (Homewood, IL: Richard D. Irwin, 1974); and Ann-Mari Sätre Åhlander, "The Environmental Situation in the Former Soviet Union," in *Environmental Problems in the Shortage Economy: The Legacy of Soviet Environmental Policy* (Cheltenham: Edward Elgar, 1994), 5–23.

32. Kornai, *The Socialist System,* 167, 169.

33. Ibid., 169.

34. Ibid., 364.

35. Ibid., 91, 95, 362–63.

36. Ibid., 91–92.

37. Ibid., 129.

38. Ibid., 498–99.

39. Ibid., 129.

40. Ibid., 109, 109n.

41. Ibid., 367, 114, 542, 116.

42. Ibid., 363.

43. Ibid., 117.

44. Marx, *Grundrisse,* 99–100.

45. Indeed, at every step of this logical construction, the concept of the vanguard party changes—just as the concepts of the commodity, money, and capital are enriched in the course of Marx's development of the concept of capital. Within a different whole, of course, the characteristics of the vanguard party may differ because of interaction with other elements in that different whole.

46. István Mészáros, *Beyond Capital: Toward a Theory of Transition* (New York: Monthly Review Press, 1995), 661.

47. Marx, *Capital,* 1:899.

48. Kornai, *Growth, Shortage and Efficiency,* 108.

49. Kornai, *Anti-Equilibrium,* 321.

50. Granick, *Enterprise Guidance in Eastern Europe,* 245–46.

51. Granick, "Central Physical Planning: Incentives and Job Rights," 149–50.

52. Hillel Ticktin stresses this point in his *Origins of the Crisis in the USSR: Essays on the Political Economy of a Disintegrating System* (Armonk, NY: M. E. Sharpe, 1992).

53. Moshe Lewin, *The Soviet Century,* 176.

54. Kornai, *Growth, Shortage and Efficiency,* 114–17.

55. Ibid., 120.

56. Kornai, *The Economics of Shortage,* 383.

57. Ibid., 212.

4. Contested Reproduction in Real Socialism

1. Kornai, *The Socialist System*, 198, 500.
2. Ibid., 366.
3. Kosolapov, *Socialism: Questions of Theory*, 463, 471-72.
4. Granick, *Enterprise Guidance in Eastern Europe*, 12-13.
5. Ibid., 11-13, 90ff. Granick dates aspects of the orthodox model back to publications in 1957, crediting among others Joseph Berliner, Holland Hunter, Alec Nove, Kornai, and himself; and he notes that the most explicit use of bonuses as the core of the model was by Sam Gindin (90n).
6. Ibid., 12, 88.
7. Donald A. Filzer, ed.,, *The Crisis of Soviet Industrialization: Selected Essays of E. A. Preobrazhensky* (White Plains, NY: M. E. Sharpe, 1979), 173.
8. Charles Bettelheim described for a subsequent period a struggle that he saw as characteristic of "transitional social formations" between the "law of value" and the "law of the social direction of the economy." Bettelheim, *Economic Calculation and Forms of Property: An Essay on the Transition between Capitalism and Socialism* (New York: Monthly Review Press, 1975), 142.
9. Evgeny Preobrazhensky, *The New Economics* (Oxford: Clarendon Press, 1965), 62-65.
10. "The immanent laws of capitalist production manifest themselves in the external movements of the individual capitals, assert themselves as the coercive laws of competition." (Marx, *Capital*, 1:433.) For development of Marx's discussion of appearance and essence in *Capital*, see Lebowitz, "What Is Competition?," in *Following Marx*, chap. 11.
11. Kornai, *The Socialist System*, 67, 169.
12. Ibid., 41.
13. Ibid., 36.
14. Kornai, *Overcentralization in Economic Administration*, 137.
15. Ibid., 215.
16. Ibid., 107.
17. Since the priority is to ensure that all units of production get their necessary inputs, it is logical that achievement of output targets be most highly rewarded—with the result that, despite bonus incentives, these additional targets tend to be viewed by managers as less important.
18. Boris Kagarlitsky, *The Dialectic of Change* (London: Verso, 1990), 250-51.
19. Flaherty, "Cycles and Crises in Statist Economies," 120.
20. Ibid., 117.
21. Åhlander, *Environmental Problems in the Shortage Economy: The Legacy of Soviet Environmental Policy*, 48-55. Åhlander draws upon the priority question to explain "the ineffectiveness of environmental programs as well as for the mismanagement of natural resources." She notes that, according to this approach, environmental disruption is the result of the priority of economic growth and that "the ineffectiveness of environmental programmes would

have been explained by their low priority in the planning and implementation of measures" (53). Obviously, under these conditions, bonuses would not be available to managers for avoiding waste and destruction of the environment.

22. Preobrazhensky, *The New Economics,* 62–65.

23. Peter Bihari, "Hungary: Toward a Socialist Market Economy?," *Studies in Political Economy* 18 (Autumn 1985), 20.

24. Kagarlitsky, *The Dialectic of Change,* 251.

25. Flaherty, "Cycles and Crises in Statist Economies," 112–13.

26. This inversion echoes Hegel's exploration of the master-slave relation—even to the point where the enterprise managers appear to embody progress. See G. W. F. Hegel, *The Phenomenology of Mind* (New York: Harper Torchbooks, 1967).

27. Under English Common Law, for example, the bundle of rights includes the right to possess, the right to the use and enjoyment of a thing, the right to decide how, when, and by whom a thing shall be used, the right to the income from the thing, the right to consume or waste the thing and the right to transmit it by sale, gift, or inheritance. Note that an individual stockholder in a capitalist corporation, for example, has the right to income from his share and the right to sell that share but does not have the right to possess, to use, to manage, or to destroy the means of production. Managers, on the other hand, possess most of those other rights but legally cannot use the means of production for their personal enjoyment. Andrew Kernohan, "Democratic Socialism and Private Property," *Studies in Political Economy,* Vol. 22, 1987:152–57.

28. Kornai, *The Socialist System,* 64–66, 98. Further, Kornai stressed that the vanguard not only has the right to the residual income but is also able to determine its extent through its power over prices, material costs, wages, and the allocation of funds; the residual income, which "is of an economic magnitude set arbitrarily by the bureaucracy," flows to the central budget, which it controls. However, despite his clear argument about the vanguard as owner, Kornai proceeded to insist that there is no real ownership in Real Socialism because real individuals do not personally benefit. "Since no one can pocket the profits and no one need pay out of his pocket for the losses, property in this sense is not only depersonalized but eliminated. State property belongs to all and to none" (73, 75). This, of course, is the standard conservative argument against all common property—including any concept of the commons organized by communities. See my comments on the commons in Lebowitz, *The Socialist Alternative,* 146–48.

29. Andras Hegedus, *Socialism and Bureaucracy* (London: Allison & Busby, 1976), 109–11.

30. Ibid., 95–96, 101.

31. Ibid., 111.

32. Ibid., 115.

33. Ibid., 117.

34. Bettelheim, *Economic Calculation*, 56.
35. Ibid., 111.
36. Ibid., 56–57.
37. Ibid., 51.
38. Ibid., 52–53.
39. Ibid., 74.
40. Hegedus, *Socialism and Bureaucracy*, 117.
41. Bettelheim, *Economic Calculation*, 75–76.
42. Ibid., 74.
43. Ibid., 74–75.
44. The vanguard party, it should be noted, also has the power to alienate the means of production by privatizing these.
45. Of course, that property right is significantly truncated. Though having a right to possess particular means of production, individuals do not have the right to direct production, choose the goal of production, sell the means of production (legally), pass these on to their children through inheritance, or exercise any other property rights besides the right of use. Nevertheless, *loss* of those job rights should be understood as a confiscation of the property rights of workers within Real Socialism.

5. *The Conductor and the Battle of Ideas in the Soviet Union*

1. Canetti, *Crowds and Power*, 460.
2. See, for example, Robert C. Allen, *Farm to Factory: A Reinterpretation of the Soviet Industrial Revolution* (Princeton: Princeton University Press, 2003). See a convenient summary of relevant points in Robert C. Allen, "A Reassessment of the Soviet Industrial Revolution," *Comparative Economic Studies* 47 (2005). As an example of the problem, in 1981 it was reported in *Voprosy Ekonomiki* that "for every rouble of basic capital there is now 28 per cent less national income." Cited in Kagarlitsky, *The Dialectic of Change*, 242.
3. Allen, "A Reassessment of the Soviet Industrial Revolution."
4. Lewin, *The Soviet Century*, 206.
5. *Current Digest of the Soviet Press* 31/29.
6. Kari T. Liuhto, "The Transformation of the Soviet Enterprise and Its Management: A Literature Review," ESRC Centre for Business Research, University of Cambridge Working Paper no. 146, 15.
7. Filzer, *Soviet Workers and the Collapse of Perestroika*, 15.
8. Lewin, *The Soviet Century*, 206-8.
9. Ibid., 210.
10. Ibid., 337–38.
11. Filzer, *Soviet Workers and the Collapse of Perestroika*, 22, 28.
12. Lewin, *The Soviet Century*, 211.
13. Ibid., 213.

14. Flaherty, "Cycles and Crises in Statist Economies," 117–18.

15. A classic example of "path dependency" is the QWERTY keyboard, which points to the great difficulty of moving on to a more efficient path once substantial resources have already been invested in a method that appeared rational at an earlier stage. See Paul A. David, "Clio and the Economics of QWERTY," *American Economic Review* (May 1985).

16. Lewin, *The Soviet Century*, 329, 216, 371.

17. *New Times* 9 (March 10, 1986): 20.

18. Lewin, *The Soviet Century*, 366.

19. Ibid., 366–67.

20. Flaherty, "Perestroika and the Soviet Working Class," 40–41.

21. Lewin, *The Soviet Century*, 367.

22. Marx, *Capital*, 3:507.

23. Kornai, *The Socialist System*, 56.

24. Canetti, *Crowds and Power*, 458.

25. J. M. Montias, "Planning with Material Balances in Soviet-Type Economies," in *Socialist Economics*, ed. Alec Nove and D. M. Nuti (Middlesex: Penguin Educational, 1974), 248.

26. Slava Gerovitch, "InterNyet: Why the Soviet Union Did Not Build a Nationwide Computer Network," *History and Technology* 24/4 (December 2008). Much of this discussion is drawn from this article.

27. Ibid.

28. Lewin, *The Soviet Century*, 218, 221.

29. Gerovitch, "InterNyet."

30. L.V. Kantorovich, "Mathematical Formulation of the Problem of Optimal Planning," in Nove and Nuti, *Socialist Economics*, 462–68.

31. Moshe Lewin, *Political Undercurrents in Soviet Economic Debates: From Bukharin to the Modern Reformers* (London: Pluto Press, 1975), 161.

32. Gerovitch, "InterNyet."

33. Ibid.

34. A. N. Kosygin, "On Improving Industrial Management," in Nove and Nuti, *Socialist Economics*, 329, 331.

35. V. V. Novzhilov, "Problems of Planned Pricing and the Reform of Industrial Management," in Nove and Nuti, *Socialist Economics*, 378–79, 383, 395.

36. Alec Nove, "Economic Reforms in the USSR and Hungary, a Study in Contrasts," in Nove and Nuti, *Socialist Economics*, 354.

37. Lewin, *Political Undercurrents in Soviet Economic Debates*, 187.

38. Nove, "Economic Reforms," 357.

39. Gerovitch, "InterNyet."

40. Kagarlitsky, *The Dialectic of Change*, 241.

41. Michael Ellman, "Economic Calculation in Socialist Economies," in *The New Palgrave: Problems of the Planned Economy*, ed. John Eatwell, Murray Milgate, and Peter Newman (New York: W. W. Norton, 1990), 99.

42. Karl Marx, "The Eighteenth Brumaire of Louis Bonaparte," in Karl Marx and Frederick Engels, *Selected Works* (Moscow: Foreign Languages Publishing House, 1951), 250.

43. Lewin, *Political Undercurrents in Soviet Economic Debates*, 180.

44. Marx, "The Eighteenth Brumaire of Louis Bonaparte," 250.

45. Lewin, *Political Undercurrents in Soviet Economic Debates*, 139, 141, 162, 166. In this work, Lewin offers a comprehensive and sympathetic presentation of the arguments of the economic reformers.

46. Ibid., 144.

47. Ibid., 164–65.

48. Ibid., 140.

49. Ibid., 171–74.

50. Ibid., 139.

51. Ibid., 157.

52. Ibid., 165–66.

53. Dobb, *Socialist Planning: Some Problems*, 45.

54. Bettelheim, *Economic Calculation and Forms of Property*, 51, 75–76.

55. Lewin, *Political Undercurrents in Soviet Economic Debates*, 210–11.

56. Ibid., 213.

57. Dobb, *Socialist Planning: Some Problems*, 13.

58. Lewin, *Political Undercurrents in Soviet Economic Debates*, 206, 209.

59. Ibid., 192.

60. Ibid., 205–6.

61. Nove, *The Soviet Economic System*, 179.

62. Lewin, *Political Undercurrents in Soviet Economic Debates*, 181, 193. Note that Lewin described many of the economists who opposed the reforms as "professors of political economy, who had built their careers on dogmas entirely divorced from economic realities" (185).

63. James P. Scanlan, "From Samazidat to Perestroika: The Soviet Marxist Critique of Soviet Society," in *The Road to Disillusion: From Critical Marxism to Post-Communism in Eastern Europe*, ed. Ray Taras (Armonk, NY: M. E. Sharpe, 1991), 24–25.

64. Scanlan, "From Samazidat to Perestroika," 26–27.

65. *New Times* 9 (March 10, 1986): 24–26.

66. Patrick Flaherty, "Perestroika and the Neoliberal Project," *Socialist Register 1991*: 148.

67. Ibid., 146; and Patrick Flaherty, "Recasting the Soviet State: Organizational Politics in the Gorbachev Era," *Socialist Register 1988*: 98.

68. Patrick Flaherty, "Perestroika and the Soviet Working Class," 44.

69. Flaherty, "Perestroika and the Neoliberal Project," 147.

70. Ibid., 148–49; Cook, *The Soviet Social Contract and Why It Failed*, 85. Such comments by intellectuals about Soviet workers were relatively mild. Mandel reports that one Soviet sociologist wrote "that the egalitarianism of

the Soviet population is nothing but 'black envy,' the ideology of lumpen, déclassé elements that make up so much of the society, a consequence of rapid industrialization and social upheaval. The ideology of the 'mass marginal' is 'leveling, destructive, malevolent envy and aggressive obedience'" David Mandel, *Perestroika and the Soviet People: Rebirth of the Labour Movement* (Montreal: Black Rose Books, 1991), 86.

71. A similar ideological victory occurred in other countries of Real Socialism although it was not only neoclassical economics as such but the "Austrian School" that influenced economists. As an example of how economic reformers ultimately embraced the capitalist entrepreneur (and concluded that only private ownership of the means of production can generate efficiency), see the discussion of Kornai and Wlodzimier Brus in Lebowitz, "The Socialist Fetter." Not surprisingly, in several countries of Real Socialism, the preferred economics textbooks became Paul Samuelson's *Economics* and even those of Milton Friedman and followers. The irony was most marked at the Karl Marx University of Economics in Budapest where the text used was Samuelson.

72. Kornai, *The Socialist System,* 41.

73. Ibid., 118–19.

74. Flaherty, "Cycles and Crises in Statist Economies," 116.

75. Ledeneva, *Russia's Economy of Favours,* 102.

6. From Moral Economy to Political Economy

1. Kornai, *Economics of Shortage,* 383.

2. Kagarlitsky, "Interview," *Against the Current.*

3. Ledeneva, *Russia's Economy of Favours,* 87. She also notes the Russian saying, "'Public' means that part of it is mine" (36).

4. Ibid., 49.

5. Ibid., 132.

6. Ibid., 167.

7. Ibid., 133.

8. Ibid., 35.

9. Ibid., 140–42.

10. E. P. Thompson, "The Moral Economy of the English Crowd in the Eighteenth Century," *Past and Present* 50 (1971): 78.

11. Li Jun, "Collective Action of Laid-off Workers and Its Implication on Political Stability: Evidences from Northeast China" (PhD diss., City University of Hong Kong, 2008), 34.

12. James C. Scott, *The Moral Economy of the Peasant: Rebellion and Subsistence in Southeast Asia* (New Haven: Yale University Press, 1976), 4–5.

13. Scott, *The Moral Economy of the Peasant,* 7.

14. Jeffrey Kopstein, "Workers' Resistance and the Demise of East Germany," http://libcom.org/history/workers-resistance-demise-east-germany-jeffrey-kopstein.

15. Thompson, "The Moral Economy of the English Crowd in the Eighteenth Century," 129.

16. Flaherty, "Recasting the Soviet State," 89–89.

17. Ivan Bernik, "Political Culture in Post-Socialist Transition: Radical Cultural Change or Adaptation on the Basis of Old Cultural Patterns?," Frankfurt Institute for Transformation Studies, No. 09, 2000.

18. Flaherty, "Perestroika and the Neoliberal Project," 145.

19. Bernik, "Political Culture in Post-Socialist Transition."

20. Efim Manevich, *Labour in the USSR: Problems and Solutions* (Moscow: Progress Publishers, 1985), 175–76.

21. Kopstein, "Workers' Resistance and the Demise of East Germany."

22. Jun, "Collective Action of Laid-off Workers," 64.

23. Bernik, "Political Culture in Post-Socialist Transition."

24. Significantly, Bernik notes that Zupanov's study of Yugoslavia indicated that both the egalitarian and authoritarian components of the egalitarian syndrome were not accepted by at least two social strata—professionals and managers.

25. Alex Pravda, "Industrial Workers and Political Development in the Soviet Union and Eastern Europe," National Council for Soviet and East European Research, 1981. http://www.ucis.pitt.edu/nceeer/1981-624-16-Pravda.pdf.

26. Sztompka cited in Bernik, "Political Culture in Post-Socialist Transition."

27. Mandel, *Perestroika and the Soviet People: Rebirth of the Labour Movement*, 37–40.

28. Pravda, "Industrial Workers and Political Development in the Soviet Union and Eastern Europe."

29. David Mandel, "Economic Reform and Democracy in the Soviet Union," *Socialist Register* 1988, 141.

30. Thompson, "The Moral Economy of the English Crowd in the Eighteenth Century," 98.

31. Ledeneva, *Russia's Economy of Favours*, 133.

32. Michael Burawoy, "Working in the Tracks of State Socialism," *Capital & Class* 98 (Summer 2009).

33. Kopstein, "Workers' Resistance and the Demise of East Germany."

34. Burawoy, "Working in the Tracks of State Socialism."

35. Thompson, "The Moral Economy of the English Crowd in the Eighteenth Century," 131.

36. Marx talked about the disintegration of a theory when it, rather than reality, is the point of departure. See Lebowitz, *Beyond CAPITAL*, 21.

37. Marx, "Value, Price and Profit," *Collected Works of Marx and Engels*, 20:143–44.

38. Ibid., 20:145.

39. Ibid., 20:148–49.

40. Marx, *Capital*, 1:675.

41. Ibid., 1:680.

42. Ibid., 1:681.
43. Ibid., 1:680.
44. Ibid., 1:682.
45. Lebowitz, *Following Marx*, 12–15; Marx, *Capital*, 3:983; Marx, *Capital*, 1:711, 713, 717, 732.
46. Lebowitz, "The Missing Book on Wage-Labour," in *Beyond CAPITAL*, 27–50.
47. Marx, *Capital*, 1:729–30, 1064; Lebowitz, *Beyond CAPITAL*, 172–74.
48. Lebowitz, *Beyond CAPITAL*, 170–77.
49. Lebowitz, *Beyond CAPITAL*, 80–81.
50. "Those who mediate among producers have an interest in maintaining and increasing the degree of separation, division and atomization among producers in order to continue to secure the fruits of cooperation in production." Lebowitz, *Beyond CAPITAL*, 99, see also 200.
51. See Lebowitz, "The Wealth of People," in *The Socialist Alternative*, chap. 1.
52. Marx, *Capital*, 1:548, 643, 799; Lebowitz, *The Socialist Alternative*, 52–55.
53. Lebowitz, *The Socialist Alternative*, 42–55.
54. Marx, *Grundrisse*, 711.
55. Marx, *Capital*, 1:772.
56. Ibid., 1:772, 375.
57. Ibid., 1:375.
58. Ibid., 1:482, 799.
59. Ibid., 1:899.
60. See the summary and deepening of this discussion in Michael A. Lebowitz, "Trapped Inside a Box? Five Questions for Ben Fine," *Historical Materialism* 18/1 (2010).
61. See the discussion of Marx's *1861–63 Economic Manuscript* in Lebowitz, "Wages," in *Beyond CAPITAL*, 101–19.
62. Marx, *Capital*, 1:793.
63. The equilibrium in this respect is the Law: "the enduring (the persisting) in appearances," as Lenin commented in his reading of Hegel. While grasping its character is an advance, Law does not go beyond the realm of appearances. See Lebowitz, *Following Marx*, 71–73.
64. Kornai, *Economics of Shortage*, 380.
65. Kornai, *Growth, Shortage and Efficiency*, 47–48.
66. Kornai, *Economics of Shortage*, 383.
67. Ibid., 509–10.
68. In 1986 I proposed that "the relation of distribution which flows from the relation of common and equal owners of the means of production is *to each according to his per capita share*." Michael A. Lebowitz, "Contradictions in the 'Lower Phase' of Communist Society," *Socialism in the World* 59 (1987): 124.
69. Marx, *Capital*, 1:681.
70. Ibid., 1:450, 548, 643, 799; Lebowitz, *The Socialist Alternative*, 52–55, 156.
71. Marx, *Capital*, 1:1064.

7. Toward a Soceity of Associated Conductors

1.   Marx, *Grundrisse*, 325; Marx, *Capital*, 1:772.
2.   Marx, *Grundrisse*, 278.
3.   Lebowitz, *Build It Now*, 67.
4.   E. P. Thompson, *The Poverty of Theory* (New York: Monthly Review Press, 1978), v.
5.   Ledeneva, *Russia's Economy of Favours*, 133.
6.   Burawoy, "Working in the Tracks of State Socialism."
7.   Cook, *The Soviet Social Contract and Why It Failed*, 3.
8.   Kopstein, "Workers' Resistance and the Demise of East Germany."
9.   See, for example, Bill Lomax, "The Working Class in the Hungarian Revolution," *Critique,* Autumn–Winter 1979–80; the Solidarnosc Program adopted in 1981 as described in *Labor Focus on Eastern Europe* 5/1–2 (Spring 1982); and "Poland: The Fight for Workers' Control," *Workers' Liberty* 10 (May 1988), excerpted from Zbigniew Kowalewski, *Rendez-nous nos usines* (Paris: PEC, 1985).
10. See Karol Kovanda, "Czechoslovak Workers' Councils," *Telos* 28 (Summer 1976).
11. Mandel, *Perestroika and the Soviet People,* 89–90, 123; Flaherty, "Perestroika and the Neoliberal Project," 151–52.
12. Lebowitz, *The Socialist Alternative*, 78–81; Marx, *Grundrisse*, 158–59, 171–72.
13. Karl Marx, *Economic and Philosophical Manuscripts of 1844,* in Marx and Engels, *Collected Works*, vol. 3 (New York: International Publishers, 1975), 296, 298.
14. Ledeneva, *Russia's Economy of Favours*, 140–42, 147.
15. Holly High, "Cooperation as Gift versus Cooperation as Corvee," paper presented at "Regenerations: New Leaders, New Visions in Southeast Asia," Council of Southeast Asian Studies, Yale University.
16. Karl Marx, "Comments on James Mill," in Marx and Engels, *Collected Works*, 3:225–28; Lebowitz, "The Solidarian Society," in *The Socialist Alternative*, 65–81.
17. Mark Osteen, "Jazzing the Gift: Improvisation, Reciprocity, Excess," *Rethinking Marxism* 22/4 (October 2010): 570.
18. Marx, *Grundrisse*, 158–59.
19. Karl Marx, *Critique of the Gotha Programme*, in Marx and Engels, *Selected Works*, vol. 2 (Moscow: Foreign Languages Publishing House, 1962), 24.
20. Marx, *Grundrisse*, 278.
21. See Lebowitz, *The Socialist Alternative*, 92–99.
22. For this discussion, see Lebowitz, "The Being and Becoming of an Organic System," in *The Socialist Alternative*, chap. 4, esp. 89–99.
23. Marx, *Capital*, 1:899.
24. Lewin, *The Soviet Century*, 363.

25. Ledeneva, *Russia's Economy of Favours,* 103.

26. Lewin, *The Soviet Century*, 365–66.

27. Lebowitz, *The Socialist Alternative*, 63–81.

28. Lebowitz, *The Socialist Alternative*, 73–76. See also the discussion of problems in Yugoslav market self-management in Lebowitz, "Seven Difficult Questions," in *Build It Now*, chap. 6.

29. Lebowitz, *The Socialist Alternative*, 77.

30. The appropriate stance was indicated by Hegel: "When we want to see an oak with all its vigour of trunk, its spreading branches, and mass of foliage, we are not satisfied to be shown an acorn instead." Indeed, that new system, "when as yet it has reached neither detailed completeness nor perfection of form, is exposed to blame on that account. But it would be as unjust to suppose this blame to attach to its essential nature, as it is inadmissible not to be ready to recognise the demand for that further development in fuller detail." G. W. F. Hegel, *The Phenomenology of Mind* (New York: Harper Torchbooks, 1967), 75, 77.

31. Karl Marx, *Theories of Surplus Value*, vol. 3 (Moscow: Progress Publishers, 1971), 84–85. See also Marx's comments about Ricardo's disciples, who attempted to solve "a series of inconsistencies, unresolved contradictions and fatuities . . . with phrases in a scholastic way. Crass empiricism turns into false metaphysics, scholasticism, which toils painfully to deduce undeniable empirical phenomena by simple formal abstraction directly from the general law, or to show by cunning argument that they are in accordance with that law." Marx, *Economic Manuscripts of 1861–63*, in Marx and Engels, *Collected Works*, vol. 30 (New York: International Publishers, 1988), 395.

32. See Lebowitz, *Following Marx*, esp. chap. 5, "Following Hegel: The Science of Marx," and chap. 10, "Marx's Methodological Method as a Whole."

33. Marx and Engels, *Collected Works*, 3:144.

34. Marx, *Grundrisse*, 278.

35. Lebowitz, *The Socialist Alternative*, 131.

8. Good-bye to Vanguard Marxism

1. Of course, Vanguard Marxism did not drop from the sky. But that is a subject for what was to be part 2 of this book and now will be part of a later book.

2. Lebowitz, *Beyond CAPITAL.*

3. Ibid., 137–38.

4. Ibid., 123.

5. Ibid., 124.

6. Ibid., 131–33, 202–4; Lebowitz, *The Socialist Alternative*, 14–16, 42–45.

7. Marx, *Capital*, 1:772, 899.

8. See, in particular, "The One-Sidedness of Wage-Labour," chap. 8, and "The Dimensions of Class Struggle," chap. 10, in Lebowitz, *Beyond CAPITAL.*

9. Ibid., 23; Karl Marx, *Economic and Philosophical Manuscripts of 1844*, in

Marx and Engels, *Collected Works*, vol. 3(New York: International Publishers, 1975), 241–42, 284.

10. Marx, *Critique of the Gotha Programme,* 24; Lebowitz, *The Socialist Alternative,* 71–72.

11. Marx, *Economic and Philosophical Manuscripts of 1844,* 241.

12. Marx, *Grundrisse,* 99–100. See the discussion of Marx's concept of an organic system in Lebowitz, *Beyond CAPITAL,* 51–59; and Lebowitz, *The Socialist Alternative,* 85–92.

13. Lukács, *History and Class Consciousness,* 27.

14. V. I. Lenin, *Philosophical Notebooks,* in Lenin, *Collected Works,* vol. 38 (Moscow: Foreign Languages Publishing House, 1961), 146–47.

15. Karl Marx and Frederick Engels, *The German Ideology,* in Marx and Engels, *Collected Works,* vol. 5 (New York: International Publishers, 1976), 53.

16. Levins and Lewontin, *The Dialectical Biologist,* 274–75.

17. Lenin, *Philosophical Notebooks,* 159.

18. The reference here is to the Sermon on the Mount which, as can be seen below, was evoked by Keynes.

19. Marx, *The Poverty of Philosophy,* 167.

20. Lenin, *State and Revolution* (Peking: Foreign Languages Press, 1965), 115–16.

21. Lenin, *State and Revolution,* 112–13.

22. In the zero-sum game of individuals exchanging their labor with society, if some are able to receive more than their contribution, others will receive less. Accordingly, the "socialist principle" is a means of regulating equal relations among owners of labor-power.

23. Lenin, *State and Revolution,* 114–15.

24. Ibid., 115.

25. Of course, it defies all logic to suggest that encouraging self-interested behavior within vanguard relations will lead to that "enormous" growth of productive forces that ushers in the society of abundance. Insofar as there is a growth of production under vanguard relations, it is *alienated* production, and the joint product is *alienated labor.* Accordingly, the need to possess alien products grows, and abundance will always be out of sight.

26. J. M. Keynes, "Economic Possibilities for our Grandchildren," *Essays in Persuasion* (New York: W. W. Norton, 1963), 358–73.

27. Marx, *Critique of the Gotha Programme,* 24.

28. Marx, *Grundrisse,* 278.

29. Ibid., 459–60. See the discussion on "the becoming of a new system" in Lebowitz, *The Socialist Alternative,* 89–99.

30. Marx, *Grundrisse,* 278.

31. Marx, *Critique of the Gotha Programme,* 23–24.

32. Ibid., 23, 25.

33. Ibid., 23.

34. Further, Marx noted *"that which is intended for the common satisfaction of needs . . .* grows in proportion as the new society develops." Ibid., 22, 24.

35. Marx, *Capital,* 3:571; Karl Marx, "Instructions to the Delegates of the Provisional General Council: The Different Questions," in *Minutes of the General Council of the First International, 1864–66* (Moscow: Foreign Languages Publishing House, n.d), 346. See Lebowitz, *Beyond CAPITAL,* 88–89; and Lebowitz, *The Socialist Alternative,* chap. 3, "The Solidarian Society," for a discussion of the limits of the cooperatives.

36. See Lebowitz, "The Production of People," chap. 2, in *The Socialist Alternative.*

37. Note, though, the essential point made by Che in his *Man and Socialism in Cuba*: "The pipe dream that socialism can be achieved with the help of the dull instruments left to us by capitalism (the commodity as the economic cell, individual material interest as the lever, etc.) can lead into a blind alley. And you wind up there after having travelled a long distance with many crossroads, and it is hard to figure out just where you took the wrong turn." Carlos Tablada, *Che Guevara: Economics and Politics in the Transition to Socialism* (Sydney, Aus.: Pathfinder, 1989), 92. I explored the problem of building upon defects at the 3rd International Conference on the Work of Karl Marx and the Challenges of the 21st Century, Havana, Cuba, May 3–6, 2006. See Michael A. Lebowitz, "Building on Defects: Theses on the Misinterpretation of Marx's Gotha Critique," *Science and Society,* October 2007.

38. Marx, "The Eighteenth Brumaire of Louis Bonaparte."

39. Efim Manevich, *Labour in the USSR* (Moscow: Progress Publishers, 1985),175–76. Is it a paradox that Vanguard Marxism's call for the enforcement of "an equal amount of products for an equal amount of labour" is the call for a fair day's pay for a fair day's work—the moral economy of the working class under capitalism?

40. Marx, *Critique of the Gotha Programme,* 25.

41. Ibid., 24–25. See also Marx, "Relations of Distribution and Relations of Production," in *Capital,* 3: chap. 51.

42. Marx, *Grundrisse,* 158–59.

43. Marx, *Capital,* vol. 3 (New York: Vintage, 1981), 959. Although Marx commented with respect to the realm of freedom that "the reduction of the working day is its basic prerequisite," this is a conception of labor within the workday as inherently alienated and separate from human development. In contrast, I have argued that, rather than reducing the workday, the point is to *transform* it into a socialist workday, which includes in its definition time for education in worker management and time for contributing to the community and household. See Lebowitz, "The Capitalist Workday, the Socialist Workday," *MRZine,* April 2008; and Lebowitz, *The Socialist Alternative,* 134, 156.

44. In *The Socialist Alternative,* I stress the importance of a political instrument to provide leadership in the struggle for socialism: "But what kind of political

instrument can build such a process? Only a party of a different type. Nothing could be more contrary to a theory that stresses the self–development of the working class through revolutionary practice than a party that sees itself as superior to social movements and as the place where the masses of members are meant to learn the merits of discipline in following the decisions made by infallible central committees" (160–61).

Index